# Tie Dip Dye

# Tie Dip Dye

## Pepa Martin and Karen Davis

A QUARTO BOOK

First edition for the United States and
Canada published in 2015 by Barron's
Educational Series, Inc.

All inquiries should be addressed to:
Barron's Educational Series, Inc.
250 Wireless Boulevard
Hauppauge, NY 11788
www.barronseduc.com

ISBN: 978-1-4380-0533-1
Library of Congress Control No: 2014930729

Conceived, designed, and produced by
Quarto Publishing plc
The Old Brewery
6 Blundell Street
London N7 9BH

QUAR.FTDP

Project editor: Chelsea Edwards
Art editor: Jackie Palmer
Designer: Simon Brewster
Photographer: Luisa Brimble
Stylist: John Mangila
Illustrator: John Woodcock
Copy editor: Ruth Patrick
Picture researcher: Sarah Bell
Proofreader: Corinne Masciocchi
Indexer: Helen Snaith
Art director: Caroline Guest
Creative director: Moira Clinch
Publisher: Paul Carslake

Color separation in Hong Kong by
Cyprus Colours (HK) Ltd
Printed in China by 1010 Printing
International Ltd

10 9 8 7 6 5 4 3 2 1

# Contents

# About this book

This book has twelve techniques, each with three variations to show that there are no hard-and-fast rules in the world of dyeing. Mix and match the different techniques, dyes, and folding formations to create uniquely beautiful pieces. In addition, every technique is accompanied by a project for you to try your hand at, from an arashi tote bag to a dip-dyed dress.

At the beginning of the book, a chapter on the essential tools and materials, as well as design placement and color considerations, will help you to get the most from the dyeing process.

**GETTING STARTED**
This chapter seeks to help you gain the best results from the dyeing process by ensuring you're equipped with the correct tools and materials. Also detailed are a number of the key dye recipes used throughout the book.

**PLEATING DIAGRAMS**
Clear diagrams demonstrate the most common folding techniques referred to in the book.

### INTRODUCTION AND TOOLS
A brief contextualization of the technique is included here, along with a list of all the tools and equipment you'll need.

### STEP-BY-STEP SEQUENCES
Concise steps are given to help you replicate each technique at home. Color photographs show you what you should be aiming for at that stage in the process.

### COLOR AND PATTERN VARIATIONS
Alongside each technique there are three examples of inspirational variations in color and pattern, which can be achieved by altering the main process slightly.

### PROJECTS
Step-by-step text is given here so that you can create beautiful items for yourself or your home. Useful tips are also featured to help you achieve the best result.

# HEALTH AND SAFETY INFORMATION

It is very important that when dealing with the harsh chemicals and dyes involved with shibori, you observe proper health and safety protocols:

- Your workspace should be in a well-ventilated area.
- Never breathe in powdered dyes or steam from any chemicals. Always wear a paper mask when dealing with dyes and you may wish to use a respirator when doing any discharging. It is best practice to bleach items outdoors.
- Do not stand over boiling pots, and use rubber gloves and an apron at all times to protect your skin.
- Keep a wet towel close at hand to quickly wipe up any spills or accidents.

It all starts with a piece of cloth and the desire to create: when you're talking tie-dye, the possibilities are endless. There is little that can go wrong and so many possibilities to explore—basic folding in one direction gets one result; fold in another and the result will be completely different. There is always a new pleat to try or a new fabric to play with, and unraveling your tied, dipped, and dyed piece is like Christmas every time.

# Why we love tie-dye

Our own journey with shibori and tie-dye began more than eight years ago. We are all about simplifying traditional techniques, oversizing designs, modifying chemicals, experimenting with fabrics, and celebrating the beauty of the imperfect.

Our love of dyeing has led us to work on some extreme projects. Never in our wildest dreams would we believe we would dip-dye a life-size hot air balloon or hand-dye fabric for Malibu surfboards. It's such a thrill when our work is used in the interiors of some of Australia's hottest night spots and commercial spaces, or we see our work on fashion runways.

We hope this book inspires you to think outside the box, to unlock your creativity, and bring out your inner child. We hope, like us, you catch the tie-dye bug, where everything you see is a potential resist and every pattern is something that can be reproduced.

Happy dyeing!

*Pepa & Karen*

Pepa Martin (left) and Karen Davis (right) in their studio in Sydney, Australia.

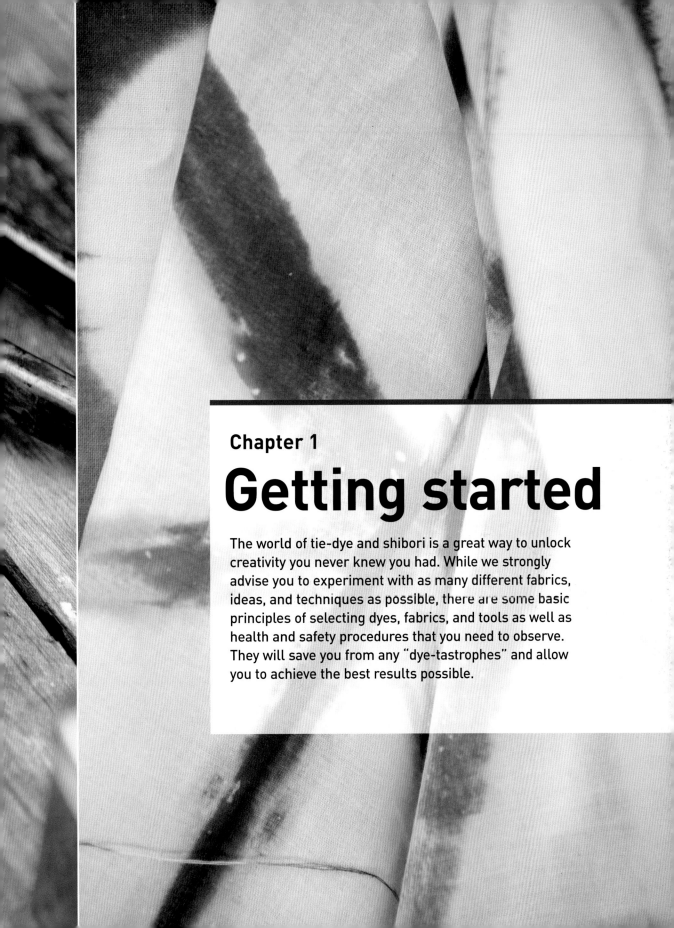

## Chapter 1

# Getting started

The world of tie-dye and shibori is a great way to unlock creativity you never knew you had. While we strongly advise you to experiment with as many different fabrics, ideas, and techniques as possible, there are some basic principles of selecting dyes, fabrics, and tools as well as health and safety procedures that you need to observe. They will save you from any "dye-tastrophes" and allow you to achieve the best results possible.

# Choosing fabrics

There are many factors that must be considered when choosing fabrics, including the fiber type, possible coating, washing process, fabric weight, and surface texture or weave.

If you already have a piece of fabric that you want to dye, this will guide your technique, as some methods will be more appropriate than others for that particular fabric. For example, linen lends itself well to bold shape-resist techniques and can leave beautiful bleed lines, while lightweight cotton voile with its tight weave is perfect for stich resist. Similarly, if you start with a technique that you want to try, this will determine the fabric types that can be used, as some will offer better outcomes. If you have a purpose, such as creating a cushion cover, this will suggest the possible fabrics and the techniques.

Certain dyes are suitable for certain fabrics and will yield the best results. You may still achieve an acceptable outcome with different dyes, but you may not get the same colorfastness or intensity. More information can be found in "Selecting dyes and recipes" (see pages 16–19).

### Natural vs. synthetic fabrics

There are three types of fibers: cellulose, which is a natural fiber and includes cotton, linen, rayon, and hemp; protein, which is an animal fiber and includes fabrics such as silk and wool; and man-made fibers, including synthetic fibers such as polyester, spandex, nylon, and acrylic. The dyer also needs to be aware of blends; if there is a synthetic component in a cellulose or protein fiber, this will affect the outcome.

There is a time and place for synthetic fabrics, and the opportunities that they offer go hand in hand with contemporary technology and pushing the boundaries of shibori. For example, polyester fabric works best when using heat-set techniques due to its thermoplastic nature. However, the handcrafted element will always complement fabrics that are natural. These fibers accept most dyes, get better results, and are overwhelmingly more beautiful to touch and work with.

### Fabric weight

Due to the nature of shibori, it's somewhat easier to begin with lightweight fabrics such as cotton voile, silks, and cheesecloth. Less effort may be required to manipulate these more manageable fabrics in certain techniques, and dye will penetrate thin materials more quickly. These are the fabrics that have been traditionally used in Japan. On the other hand, while dye may take longer to soak into thicker or heavier fabrics, it may be more suitable for your desired application, such as upholstery or heavy curtain fabric. The size of your piece will also be a determining factor in the resist technique

## Presoaking

It is recommended that you presoak your fabric before dyeing to ensure even dye penetration. Since cloth can shrink once wet, it is possible that the resists you have applied tightly will become loose and therefore not be able to fulfill their role in resisting dye. Presoaking minimizes this risk. Also, water acts as a temporary barrier for your dye that forces it to soak up slowly, which means it is less likely to penetrate the area that is supposed to resist the dye, creating stronger dye lines. Heavier fabrics will need to be soaked for longer periods of time.

chosen. Very labor-intensive techniques, such as stitch-resist patterns, may be more suitable to smaller pieces or as placement designs.

### PFD fabrics

You are able to buy fabrics specifically made for printing or dyeing. These are often known as PFD fabrics (prepared for dyeing). These will have no coating on them and are often found in fabric stores. These are best for beginners, as no fabric preparation is required.

Linen (1), cotton (2), silk organza (3), cotton voile (4), burlap (5), cotton (6)

# Selecting dyes and recipes

Choosing the right dye for your fabric will produce the best result. This is the part where your inner scientist has time to shine (you may not think you have it in you until you realize how exciting it is to mix colors). Be sure to test your dye on a small piece of cloth, as this will give you an indication of the final result.

The majority of dyes used in this book are fiber-reactive or acid dyes. You can achieve great results with all of the techniques using the more commonly available direct dyes, but the outcomes will be less vibrant and colorfast.

### Fiber-reactive dyes

These dyes are normally used to dye fabrics made of cellulose fibers, such as cotton, linen, and rayon. Fiber-reactive dyes can be used to dye silk or wool, but the color will not be as strong. These dyes should not be used with synthetic materials, as they will not stay fixed to the fabric. A fiber-reactive dye is very easy to use and has great colorfastness. They are also known as cold-water dyes; however, it is easier to dissolve these dyes in hot water (no warmer than 105°F [40°C]), so this name is a little misleading. These dyes require soda ash in order for the dye to be fixed to the fabric. Table salt or urea is often added to aid dye penetration and help it color evenly (the quantities you should add will be included in the manufacturer's instructions).

### Direct dyes

Direct dyes are the most common form of dye available for home dyeing and can often be found at the supermarket or drugstore. They are for use on cellulose fabrics but offer the least colorfastness of all dyes. Direct dyes yield the best result when used in boiling water with the addition of salt. Direct dyes often already contain soda ash, so no extra is required.

It is important that when you are laundering items that have been dyed with direct dyes, you sort and wash them with like colors and in cold water only.

### Acid dyes

Acid dyes are used for protein fibers such as silk, wool, and nylon. These are also known as hot-water dyes, as they must be dissolved in almost boiling water in order to be able to fix color. When dyeing protein fibers, you will need a mildly acidic dye bath in order to fix the dye to the fiber. We use vinegar, a mild acid, to lower the pH of the dye bath. Acid dyes cannot be used with synthetic materials, as they will not react.

### Synthetic dyes

Synthetic dyes are used for man-made fibers such as polyester. Be aware of fabric blends, as using fiber-reactive or acid dyes with cloth that is blended with a man-made material may give patchy results, depending on the synthetic percentage. In the case of a mixed fiber fabric—for example, 90% polyester and 10% cotton—the fabric will need to be dyed twice: once with a polyester dye and once with a dye suitable for cotton.

### Soda ash

Soda ash is also known as sodium carbonate or washing soda. It is a mild alkaline and raises the pH level of the liquid that the fabric is in. A high pH level is required in order for fiber-reactive dye to fix to fabric.

There are a number of ways to use soda ash. Sometimes, soda ash is dissolved in hot water and fabrics are presoaked in this solution before the dyeing process begins. This is the same process as degumming, in which the protective layer of silk organza—the sericin or silk gum—is removed, giving the fabric a smoother texture.

At other times, soda ash is mixed with a dye concentrate. It is not used with all dye types and is most commonly used with fiber-reactive dyes. Soda ash can also be used to remove color in some techniques. Always read the manufacturer's instructions for directions. These will include information on weighing your fabric, which dictates the amount of soda ash you should use.

Soda ash is used because it is nontoxic and eco-friendly. That said, it is still a chemical, and it is important to wear a mask and rubber gloves at all times to avoid breathing in vapors and to protect your skin and lungs.

### Indigo dye

Indigo dye is derived from a plant and is the traditional dye used in Japanese shibori. There is natural indigo and man-made or synthetic indigo. You are more likely to produce stronger shades more quickly with synthetic indigo. Indigo is a vat dye, and the process makes you feel like an alchemist.

Your vat needs to be protected from the elements and, if treated with care, will last for several months  The indigo vat will never become clear and be exhausted of color. When the bath is in its green state, this indicates that the dye bath is reduced and is ready to dye the fabric. It will only turn from this healthy green color to a blue color if it has been accidentally oxidized (you want the oxidation to happen on your cloth instead).

Acid dye (1 and 2), indigo dye (3),
fiber-reactive dye (4), direct dye (5)

However, there are several factors to be taken into consideration when working with indigo. Indigo powder cannot be dissolved in water alone but must be used in conjunction with other chemicals in order to become water soluble. The blue indigo powder must undergo a chemical change in the vat to become water soluble. This makes it go green. When fabric is removed from the dye vat, the indigo oxidizes and reverts to its insoluble form—turning blue. Follow the manufacturer's instructions to make up your indigo dye vat, as recipes differ.

Unlike fiber-reactive and acid dyes that penetrate into fabric, indigo dye sits on the surface. This makes it a great dye for beginners, as it gives instant results and beautiful textures. Just like your blue jeans, the color will rub off, so be careful. Don't wash items dyed using indigo with regular clothing detergent, as the soda ash contained in it will remove more of the color. To prevent this, wash these items with dishwashing liquid. Exposing indigo to the sun will fade the color. It is hard to fail with indigo—the color is vibrant and is stunning in every form. Synthetic indigo has been used in this book, as it is simpler to prepare for the uninitiated dyer.

### Removing color
You can also take color out of cloth and, in doing so, reverse the typical dyeing process. Techniques will be followed as usual, but with a decolorant rather than dye, so that you are removing the color from the area you would normally be dyeing. Fabrics need to be predyed because of this.

There are three main chemicals that can be used to remove color: discharge powder, bleach, and soda ash. Discharge chemicals such as thiourea dioxide and sodium hydrosulphite can be made up as a bath or as a paste and applied to cloth. These chemicals work slowly and are the least harmful to the cloth of the decolorants. Silk can only be discharged in this way using sodium formaldehyde sulphoxylate. Bleach works very quickly but is incredibly harsh, and some materials, such as silk, would simply deteriorate if you used bleach with them. A bleach-stopping aid must be used to inhibit the bleach from continuing to eat away at your cloth. The safest way to neutralize bleach (for the cloth as well as for the dyer) is by using sodium bisulfite or sodium metabisulfite. Sodium bisulfite chemically "couples up" with the chlorine molecule, neutralizing its effect. Hydrogen peroxide and vinegar should not be used as bleach-stopping agents, as they will combine with the bleach to create harmful chlorine gas. In large quantities, soda ash can also work as a decolorant. Again, this is only possible on certain fabrics and using certain dyes, such as direct dyes.

As with every other aspect of shibori, consider your materials and the outcome you desire before choosing which decolorant to utilize.

### Natural dyes
Using natural dyes is a whole new world where color can be made from what you have in the garden or kitchen. Beautiful patterns can be achieved in natural, earthy tones. However, the process of setting natural dyes sometimes requires very toxic chemicals. This type of dye requires people who love the art of science.

### Dye-to-fabric ratio
It is important to clearly read your dye manufacturer's instructions to find out the amount of dye needed for the weight of fabric. If you find that your dye water stays very dark after the dyeing process, you are probably using too much dye.

### Washing after dyeing
When washing fabric after dyeing, be sure to use a delicate laundry detergent free from harsh discoloring agents. This will remove any excess dye and maintain the strongest color and protect your precious resist work. There are specialty chemicals, such as synthropal, that are available to make sure that no residual dye particles remain on your fabric. However, it is also possible to use regular dishwashing liquid as an alternative for home dyers.

# Dye recipes

Throughout the book these dye recipes are referred to.

### Synthetic indigo
Fill up a tub with 4 gallons (15 L) of warm water. Sprinkle in your indigo powder and sodium hydrosulfite. Stir gently. Dissolve your soda ash in 2 tablespoons (30 ml) of hot water. Slowly add this solution to the dye vat. Leave for 15 minutes.

### Acid dye
Fill up a tub with 4 gallons (15 L) of water per 17 oz (500g) of dry fabric. Dissolve your acid dye in just enough boiling water to make a solution. Add ½ teaspoon of vinegar for every 2 pints (1 L) of water. Stir thoroughly.

### Fiber-reactive dye
Fill the tub with 4 pints (2 L) warm water for every 3½ ounces (100 g) of dry fabric. Dissolve the fiber-reactive dye in just enough warm water to make a solution. Add it to your dye tub. Dissolve salt and soda ash in hot water (for every 4 pints [2 L] of water you'll need 2¾ ounces [80g] of salt and 1 ounce [30g] of soda ash) and add to your tub. Stir.

### Bleach neutralizing solution
Add 1 tablespoon of sodium metabisulfite to 2½ gallons (10 L) of water.

### Degumming using soda ash
Dissolve ⅓ ounce (10 g) of soda ash in 4 pints (2 L) of boiling water in an old bucket.

| Dye type | Material | Guidelines |
| --- | --- | --- |
| Direct dye | Cotton and viscose | Dissolve dye in boiling water, soak fabric in soaking bucket for 15 minutes, wring out, and add to dye tub. Dye fabric in boiling water with addition of table salt for 30 minutes. Rinse in cold water. |
| Acid dye | Wool | Add your presoaked wool to the dye pot. Bring the temperature slowly up to boiling point. Add vinegar (amounts detailed on dye packet). Stir and leave just below boiling point for 30 minutes, stirring regularly. Remove from dye pot and leave to sit for 10 minutes to cool down. Wash in warm water. |
| | Silk and nylon | Dissolve dye in boiling water (do not use water hotter than 185°F [85°C] when dyeing silk), bring water to boiling point, then add dye and acetic acid. Soak fabric in soaking bucket for 15 minutes before adding to dye tub. Dye for 15 to 30 minutes (leave for 45 to 60 minutes for darker shades). Rinse in cold water. |
| Fiber-reactive dye | Cotton, linen | Dissolve dye in warm water and, when cool, add water to dye pot. Add dissolved cooking salt to the dye pot. Soak fabric in soaking bucket for 10 minutes before adding to dye tub. Add cloth to dye tub and leave for 10 minutes. Dissolve soda ash and add to dye tub. Leave for another 60 to 90 minutes. Remove and rinse in cold water, then wash in hot water (140°F [60°C]), and rinse once more in cool water. If the final rinse water does not run clear, repeat the hot wash and cool rinse. |
| Indigo dye | Wool, cotton, silk linen | Prepare your synthetic indigo vat. Leave for the time allocated on your manufacturer's instructions. Soak fabric in soaking bucket for 10 minutes. Wring out and put in vat for 15 minutes. Remove from vat without creating bubbles. Leave to oxidize for 10 minutes. Rinse until water runs clear. Wash with dishwashing liquid and rinse again. |
| Synthetic dye | Polyester and nylon | Fill dye tub with water and polyester dye and stir. Add fabric and dye for 30 to 60 minutes at boiling point. |
| Removing color (Thiourea dioxide recipe) | Linen, cotton dyed with fiber-reactive and direct dyes | Soak your predyed and bound fabric in a soaking bucket of water. Dissolve 1 teaspoon of soda ash in 3½ fluid ounces (100 ml) of hot water in a pot large enough to hold just over 4 pints (2 L) of water. Add 4 pints (2 L) of water and bring to boil. Once boiled, add ¼ teaspoon of thiourea dioxide, stirring slowly as you go. Add fabric, simmer for 20 to 30 minutes. Remove and allow to cool. Wash in warm water with dishwashing liquid. |
| Bleaching | Burlap, denim | Presoak your fabric item in a bucket of water. Make up your bleach solution: 2¼ gallons (9 L) of water to 1 cup (250 ml) of household bleach. Submerge your presoaked piece into the bleach mix and leave until you reach the desired result (approximately 2 hours). Remove from bleaching vessel and rinse thoroughly. Mix up your bleach neutralizing solution: 1 tablespoon of sodium metabisulfite to 2½ gallons (10 L) of water. Soak your piece for 2 hours, remove, and re-rinse. |

Polyester thread (1), sewing pins (2), toothpicks (3), rubber gloves (4), measuring spoons (5), resists (6 and 8), clamps (7 and 11), marbles (9), rubber bands (10)

# Selecting tools

When selecting your tools, it is important to consider their size, their capacity to fulfill their functional role, and the material they are made of.

Vessels must be large enough to fit the required amount of dye and water (if necessary) as well as the entire fabric piece with space to move, potentially including resists such as poles or clamps.

Dye tubs could be large stainless-steel saucepans or plastic tubs, as these won't rust—grab any old pots or buckets that have seen better days and give them a new purpose. Plastic buckets are good for cold-water dyes, and when using techniques that require heat or the cooktop, you will need a metal pot. Make sure you're using nonreactive metal pots and pans, such as enamel or stainless steel. Aluminum pots will dull colors.

All tools must be able to withstand the chemicals with which they will be coming into contact. In some cases, you will be directed to use synthetic twine, as nonsynthetic twine will absorb the dye and not act as a resist.

Once a tool or vessel has been used for dyeing, it must not be used for anything else again. Source an appropriate tub and label it "Dyeing," and store all tools and chemicals within this so that nothing is accidentally used in the kitchen or elsewhere in the home.

A resist item (see page 22) should be the shape and size that you desire for your pattern, and the tools (such as string or clamps) must have the strength and tension to hold these items in place. Find anything around the house and try it out. These could be any two things that are the same shape, such as old tiles, rulers, jar lids, pegs, or cooking utensils. You should not need to buy anything new for these techniques. Soon you will be considering everything in your home to be a potential resist!

While shibori is a super-fun activity, don't forget that you're working with hazardous chemicals and you should always exercise good practice when it comes to health and safety. See page 9 for more information on working safely.

Plumber's pipe (1), saucepan (2), ruler (3), rope (4), scissors (5), heavy plastic twine (6), bamboo steamer (7)

# Folding and clamping fabric

There are so many ways to translate shibori onto your cloth. You have the power to plan your design, and there is nothing stopping you from thinking outside the box—but it is important to consider basic design elements. This involves playing with scale, direction, and tone.

There are so many exciting techniques and colors to try, and often the hardest thing to do is to keep it simple. It is a good idea to record your shibori process through photos and a visual diary so that you will always remember how to create a pattern.

The concept of planning a design comes down to the resist technique you are using: this is the way you fold and hold your fabric together before it is dyed. Pleats are about folding cloth in certain ways and securing them to create a resist. The folds stop dye from penetrating through the entire cloth and remain undyed, the pleat forms the repeat, and the consequence is a beautiful shibori pattern. The way in which the pleat is held, whether it is with clamps or string, will add to the design and allow for further variations. No matter how simple or complex, every fold has the power to create a story on your cloth.

Appreciate positive and negative space—the areas that are not dyed are just as important as those that are. They may offer a moment of serenity in untouched, white cloth that works to highlight a simple, beautiful strip of shibori on one end. You may wish to cover the whole piece in a repeat pattern, or discharge a design into already colored fabric. In this way, placement is essential and has the power to transform the mood of your final piece.

Considering space and placement in your design plan could include dyeing an area that is off-center, altering your symmetry, and playing with size. All of these things are what makes a piece of hand-dyed cloth truly your own creation.

Shibori uses a series of pleats to create organized repeats. The pleat can be used to create different effects or textures within your resists. One of the most common pleats used in shibori is the accordion pleat. Folding the fabric back and forth in an "accordion" or "concertina"-like manner ensures that the fabric is always on the outside as opposed to rolling in on itself, which buries the inner layers. Other pleats to experiment with are step pleats, in which the fabric is pleated in one direction and the pleats sit next to each other with space in between. This space is your exposed area, which, when bound, will display your pattern, and the hidden step forms a dye barrier or another level of resistance. Pleating is another way to add a sophisticated repeat to your shibori experience. Combining pleating with stitching takes your design to a whole new level, and experimenting further with pleats will offer you unlimited possibilities.

ACCORDION
PLEATS

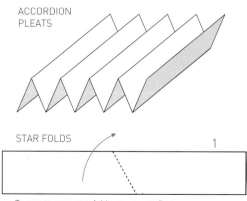

STAR FOLDS

1

To create your star folds, you must, first, accordion pleat your fabric. Fold your length of fabric beginning in the center at the angle shown above.

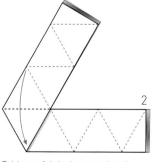

Fold your fabric downward so that you are creating equilateral triangles as you fold.

Fold your fabric across continuing to create equilateral triangles until you are left with a triangular stack.

Household pegs (1), plastic twine (2), resist shapes (3), rubber band (4)

Heat-set pleats on polyester fabric (1), bound fabric on mixed fibers (2), bound fabric on cotton (3)

# Color

Color wheels, palettes, and moodboards are wonderful tools, but when it comes down to it, color is subjective, and your aesthetic will determine what you are attracted to. As artists, we tend to move toward tertiary and moody colors because, to us, they create subtle pieces that echo the way in which they were created—by hand.

Drawing designs and noting color schemes are a great way of working up ideas before committing material and dyes.

Bright, rich colors are often associated with tie-dye, and these might be the tones that make your heart soar. But there is always more to the color than simply the color choice itself. If you are utilizing the ombré technique, there will be a gradation of the same color, and in the scrunch technique, a vast array of different tones will be revealed. Most techniques will provide a number of tones due to the perfect inconsistencies of hand dyeing. Over time, you will have the skill to manipulate the strength of the tone and mix colors so that you are more likely to get exactly what you want. With practice and confidence, most aspects of shibori can be played with, manipulated, and adapted.

It is important to consider the reality of bleeding dye lines. These create incredible textural aspects to a cloth but may be disappointing if colors are placed too closely together and mix with one another. Yellow and blue dyes will give you green—all of the same color theory rules you learned in art class apply when dyeing fabric. Think about whether this should be avoided, adapt your resists accordingly, and choose colors carefully.

Don't forget that the color of the dye powder is rarely the color of the dye. Also, the color will always be lighter once the piece is dry—so allow your shades to become darker during the wet dyeing process.

Consider your color palette, the purpose of the dyed cloth, and the space in which it will exist. Color combined with pattern creates the mood of your fabric. A gray stripe might be a strong statement, whereas a gray scrunch can be soft and delicate. Think about the story that you want it to tell, and choose your color with intent.

### Some basic color theory

Primary colors are red, yellow, and blue. They are colors that can't be created by mixing other colors. When they are mixed together, they create secondary colors.

Warm colors, such as red, yellow, and orange, are bright and energetic. Cool colors, such as blue and green, give the impression of calm and are soothing to the eye. While warm colors tend to advance, cool colors look as if they are receding. All of these are important factors to consider when working on a design. White, black, and gray are neutral shades. Neutral colors are great to use alongside strong colors in order to tone them down or can be used alone to create subtle designs.

When you are working with dyes, you will find premade dyes of these colors readily available to you. Often the powder form does not resemble the final dyed outcome, so it's a good idea to do test swatches of all your colors. Once you have these colors, you can experiment with mixing shades to make your own unique color palette. It's a good idea to keep a diary of your dye recipes for future experimentation. Color can open up a whole new world, and mixing dye colors can be just as fun as making shibori patterns.

Secondary colors are green, orange, and purple. They are made up by mixing combinations of red, yellow, and blue.

Red + Yellow = Orange
Yellow + Blue = Green
Blue + Red = Purple

Tertiary colors are made up from the mixing of combinations of both primary and secondary colors.

For example:
Orange + Yellow = Warm Yellow
Red + Orange = Warm Red
Red + Purple = Cool Red
Blue + Purple = Cool Blue
Blue + Green = Warm Blue
Yellow + Green = Warm Green

Each pair of linen swatches has been dyed with a fiber-reactive dye at full strength and at 35% strength.

## Chapter 2

# Techniques and projects

The beauty of tie-dye and modern shibori is that there are endless possibilities. With a little bit of know-how and a lot of imagination, you have the ability to create something beautiful and one of a kind.

All the techniques and projects in this book have evolved from things learned, mastered, and tinkered with. Every project and technique can be reinterpreted in millions of different ways, and a different outcome can be as simple as changing the fabric, dye, size, or placement of your resist, or stitches. There are no right or wrong outcomes, only exploration and experimentation.

While some techniques have a strong grounding in traditional Japanese shibori, others are inspired by the liberating notion of tie-dye. Feel free to mix and match, and be confident and have fun, for your tie-dye adventure begins now!

# Ombré
## Dip-dyeing

Dip-dye, otherwise known as ombré, is a dyeing technique in which shades of color graduate from light to dark. Commonly used in fashion and interiors, this simple technique has the ability to add subtle sophistication to fabric. Depending on the color used, dip-dye can appear soft and elegant, or dramatic and eye catching.

3

Dip-dyeing can be done in a multitude of ways. The artist must first decide the desired outcome for this delicate finish, as the feel can be drastically changed depending on a number of factors.

For example, the placement of the darkest tone will totally change the impact of the piece. If the darkest tone is placed at the bottom and lightens as it rises up the piece, the effect is uplifting and feminine. If the tones are reversed and the darkest tone is at the top, the opposite effect is created. If the darkest tone is placed in the middle and lightens outward, a dramatic effect is created, emphasizing an area and creating a focal point. The dark tone will attract attention and can be used as a tool depending on the purpose of the piece. In fashion, it can be used to accentuate body shape. The size of the dark tone and the range of color will transform the fabric. Very dark with little range will create heaviness, whereas dark with an extensive range requires much attention but lightens the piece significantly. Having the darkest tone as a midtone will transform the result to be soft and subtle, whether there is an extensive range or not. Introducing multiple points of gradation, slowly moving through monochromatic tones, will give a sense of movement to a piece and can add natural texture that is far from planned.

Though dip-dyeing may seem quite a simple process, creating a seamless gradation of tone is much harder than it first appears. The fabric must constantly be lifted up and down so no clear banding lines appear. Successful dip-dyeing requires precision and patience, but is well worth the effort.

4

## you will need

White or lightly colored cotton fabric (1)

Soaking bucket

Dye tub (2)

Rubber gloves

Paper mask

Direct dye (3)

Three glass jars (4)

Coat hanger with a horizontal bar or a piece of dowel

# How to create a gradated dip-dye

**1** Soak the piece of fabric in a bucket of water for 15 minutes. Remove the fabric from the bucket, wringing out the excess water, then fill the dye tub with warm water.

**2** Dissolve the direct dye in 1 pint (500 ml) of warm water. Distribute the dye concentrate equally into three jars. The dye in the jars is all the same concentration and is diluted when poured into the dye bath. The principle of submersion dyeing is that the dye is used up when the water has run clear. This method works by layering the color so that the bottom layer will have all three levels, hence the darker pigmentation.

Pour one jar of dye into the water in the dye tub.

**3** Hang the top of the fabric from a coat hanger or dowel. This area will remain white and therefore will not be entering the dye bath.

**4** Submerge three-quarters of the fabric in the dye bath. Leave for 20 minutes, agitating regularly.

**5** Raise one-quarter of the fabric out of the dye bath. It may be easier to suspend the hanger from a chair or low table. Pour in the second jar of dye, ensuring that you do not pour directly onto the fabric. Leave for 20 minutes, agitating regularly.

**6** Lift the fabric again, leaving only the bottom quarter in the dye bath.

**7** Pour in the third jar of dye concentrate, ensuring that you do not pour it directly onto the fabric. Leave for 20 minutes, agitating regularly.

**8** Carefully remove your fabric from the dye bath. It is important not to mark the white areas with dye. Rinse with cold water running away from the white section. Rinse until the water runs clear.

# 1 Stripes

**Adding ombré effects gives dimension to basic stripes.**

Iron your cloth and accordion pleat it as if you were creating basic stripes (see page 48). The pleat defines the size of your stripe. Hold your pleats together with clamps and place the fabric in a soaking bucket for 10 minutes. Fill your dye tub with 2 pints (1 L) of warm water. Prepare your fiber-reactive dye as per the instructions on page 18. Pour approximately ¾ inch (2 cm) of the dye into a shallow dye tub. This will be your darkest section of stripe.

Remove the cloth from the bucket and dab the excess water with a towel. Holding the clamps, drape the edge of your pleats into the dye tub and leave for 15 minutes. Then add warm water to the dye tub to lift the water level an extra 2 inches (5 cm) and leave for 15 minutes. This will dilute your dye and give you a lighter shade. If you wish, you can add smaller amounts of water and increase the level of gradation. Refer to the instructions for the total dye time required to ensure each color level has time to set. Once the dye process is complete, remove the fabric without getting the white area in the dye, rinse, remove the clamps, and rinse again.

# 2 Circle

**By isolating an area on your fabric, you can create a dip-dye focal point.**

Lay your fabric on a flat surface. Using your thumb and index finger, pinch the center of your fabric into a peak. Maintaining the pinch, run your other hand down the fabric and then stop at the desired size of your dip-dye circle. Place a rubber band at this point to secure.

Soak this area to just above the rubber band for 10 minutes. Wring out. Fill a small dye tub with 4 pints (2 L) of water per 3½ oz (100 g) of dry fabric. Prepare your fiber-reactive dye as per the instructions on page 18.

Holding the fabric securely at the base of the rubber band, submerge your full gathered circle. Leave for 2 minutes or until there is a light shade of color. Raise one-quarter of the dipped fabric and leave for 10 minutes. Raise another quarter and leave for another 20 minutes or until the water is colorless (this will give you the darkest shade possible). This is known as exhausting the dye tub.

# 3 Two ends

**Dip-dyeing from the top and bottom accentuates the center of the fabric.**

Fold your fabric in half and place in a soaking bucket for 10 minutes. Fill your dye tub with 2 pints (1 L) of warm water. Prepare your fiber-reactive dye as per the instructions on page 18. Remove your fabric from the soaking bucket and wipe off the excess water with a towel.

Drape the fabric over a hanger so both sides are equally aligned. Fill your dye tub with approximately 4 inches (10 cm) of warm water and stir in the dye concentrate. Lower the hanger so the ends of your fabric are submerged (this will be the darkest shade). Move the fabric to spread the dye evenly, being careful not to splash the white area. Leave for 15 to 20 minutes. Add warm water, raising the water level an extra 2 to 4 inches (5 to 10 cm). This will dilute the dye concentrate and give the lighter shade. Agitate the fabric to spread the dye evenly.

Once the dye process is complete, carefully remove the fabric. Rinse until the water runs clear, and leave on the hanger to dry to ensure your white stays white!

# Project: Dip-dye summer dress

Dip-dye (or ombré) is a great way to embellish your favorite summer dress. Adding simple color gradation is elegant, individual, and a great way to turn an everyday dress into a one-of-a-kind dress.

Remember: When dip-dyeing, it is important to keep the area of the dress you would like to remain white out of the way of the dye to avoid marks or spills.

1 Place your cotton dress in a soaking bucket for 15 to 30 minutes. Prepare your fiber-reactive dye by dissolving it in just enough warm water to make a solution.

2 Remove your dress from the soaking bucket and wring out. Place the dress on a coat hanger.

3 Fill your dye tub with approximately 10 inches (25 cm) of warm water and stir in the dye concentrate. Lower the dress so that the bottom third is submerged (this will be the darkest shade). Move the dress to spread the dye evenly, being careful not to splash the white area. Dissolve salt in hot water and add to dye bath. Dissolve soda ash in hot water and add to dye bath (see fiber-reactive recipe on page 18 for guidance on amounts). Leave for 15 to 20 minutes, agitating regularly.

4 Add warm water, raising the water level an extra 10 inches (25 cm) or as high as you would like the ombré effect. This will dilute the dye concentrate and give a lighter shade. Agitate the fabric to spread the dye evenly.

5 After another 20 minutes, carefully remove the dress from the dye tub. Rinse until the water runs clear and leave on the hanger while drying to ensure your white stays white!

## Dip-dye tips

Fiber-reactive dyes work best on cotton and linen fabrics. If your dress is made out of silk or wool, follow these steps using acid dye.

Deciding the best area to dip-dye depends on your dress. For a long maxi dress, you may decide to highlight the length by dip-dyeing only the bottom; however, it might be interesting to dye the midsection as a feature.

# Arashi Pole wrapping

"Arashi" is the Japanese word for storm—the traditional version of this technique resembles heavy rain in a storm. The playful nature of arashi opens the imagination to the countless possibilities of tie-dye.

Arashi uses a long pole and fabric compression to form a resist that leaves stripes on the fabric. The fabric is wrapped around the pole in a specific way (in order to achieve the desired pattern), fixed into place with rubber bands, and squashed as far as possible to one end of the pole. The pole is then submerged in a dye bath. Wrapping the fabric in different ways will produce different patterns.

The traditional form of arashi involves wrapping the fabric at a 45-degree angle to the pole, creating a diagonal stripe. There have been many modifications to modernize this technique that vary the size, direction, and scale of the stripes, according to the way the fabric is wrapped around the pole, the angle at which it is wrapped, whether the fabric is pleated before wrapping, and much more.

The beauty of arashi is in its movement. It portrays impressions of water, such as a choppy ocean or stormy sky, and the powerful emotions that these images evoke. The patterns are striking, organized but organic in design, and with an element of the unknown that is always in play when working with shibori.

By far one of the most fascinating techniques, pole wrapping or arashi shows that the world of dyeing has much to offer.

2

3

6

## you will need

Iron

Strip of white or lightly colored cotton approximately 12 inches (30 cm) wide (1)

*NOTE:* The size of your fabric is determined by the diameter of your plastic plumbing pipe. If you want to dye a larger piece of fabric, you will need a wider pole.

Approximately 20 inches (50 cm) of plastic plumbing pipe 4 inches (10 cm) in diameter (2)

Rubber bands (3)

Soaking bucket

Towel

Paper mask

Rubber gloves (4)

4

Dye vat large enough to submerge your plumbing pipe

Spoon (5)

Indigo dye (6)

Small scissors (7)

Sodium hydrosulfite

Soda ash

2

3

# How to tie-dye using pole wrapping

**1** Iron the piece of fabric, then lay it down on a hard surface.

**2** Place the plumbing pipe diagonally on top of the fabric with one end of the pole positioned in the top corner. Wrap the fabric over the pole, ensuring that the two edges of fabric meet up but do not overlap. Any overlapping fabric will cause a ghosting or masked-out effect on your pattern.

**3** Secure the fabric around both ends of the pipe with rubber bands.

**4** Wrap rubber bands around the pipe at approximately ¾-inch (2-cm) intervals. Make sure they are tight enough to resist the dye, and double over if necessary.

**5** Push the fabric down hard to compress the fabric between the bands. This compression is what creates your resist.

**6** Soak the pipe in a bucket of water for 15 minutes. Remove the pipe from the water and dab the excess water with a towel.

**7** Prepare your synthetic indigo vat by filling up a tub with 4 gallons (15 L) of warm water. Sprinkle in your indigo powder and sodium hydrosulfite. Stir gently. Dissolve your soda ash in 2 tablespoons (30 ml) of hot water. Slowly add this solution to the dye vat. Leave for 30 minutes. Submerge the wrapped pipe in the dye tub and leave for 15 minutes; do not agitate.

**8** Rinse under cold water until the water runs clear. Remove the rubber bands from the pipe; sometimes it's easier and more time-effective to cut the bands off using small scissors. Rinse the fabric again until the water runs clear.

## 1 Degum

Degumming silk organza adds an opaque effect to a sheer material.

Iron your fabric on a flat surface and accordion pleat it at approximately 3 inches (7.5 cm). Place your strip of pleated fabric horizontally on the table and place the plumbing pipe diagonally across the fabric. Roll the fabric diagonally along the pipe and secure both ends with rubber bands.

Place rubber bands down the pipe, compressing the fabric as you go. Place the fabric in a soaking bucket for 20 minutes. Remove and squeeze out the water.

Prepare your soda ash solution as per the instructions on page 18. Submerge the silk on the plumbing pipe into your hot soda ash solution. Leave for 30 minutes.

Remove the pipe from the dye tub and rinse under cold water. Release the silk from the pipe. Add 2 tablespoons of white vinegar to a bucket of water and neutralize the silk for 10 minutes. Wring out and hang out to dry.

## 2 Straight

Using arashi on a horizontal line instead of a diagonal creates the feel of a calm ocean rather than a storm.

Lay your fabric on a flat surface and iron out any creases. Roll your fabric straight around the plumbing pipe and secure both ends with rubber bands.

Place rubber bands down the length of the pipe, compressing the fabric as you go. Place the fabric in a soaking bucket for 20 minutes. Prepare your synthetic indigo vat as per the instructions on page 18. Remove the pipe from the soaking bucket and wring out the excess water. Submerge the wrapped pipe in the dye tub and leave for 15 minutes; do not agitate.

Remove the pipe from the dye tub and allow it to oxidize for 15 minutes. Rinse under cold water. Then release the fabric from the pipe and rinse until the water runs clear.

## 3 Chevron

A textural and random V-shaped pattern that produces unexpected results when using arashi.

Lay your fabric on a flat surface and iron. Accordion pleat your fabric at approximately 3-inch (7.5-cm) intervals. Place your strip of pleated fabric horizontally on the table and place the plumbing pipe diagonally across the fabric. Roll the fabric diagonally along the pipe and secure both ends with rubber bands.

Place rubber bands down the length of the pipe, compressing the fabric down as you go. Place the fabric in a soaking bucket for 20 minutes. Prepare your synthetic indigo vat as per the instructions on page 18. Remove the pipe from the soaking bucket and wring out the excess water. Submerge the wrapped pipe in the dye tub and leave for 30 minutes; do not agitate.

Remove the pipe from the dye tub and allow it to oxidize for 15 minutes. Rinse under cold water. Then release the fabric from the pipe and rinse under cold water.

# Project: Arashi tote bag

The beautiful feathery lines of arashi are a great texture to dress up your tote or shopping bag.

If you are using a muslin shopping or tote bag, it's a good idea to soak it in boiling water to remove the coating that is commonly found on the fabric.

1 Prewash your tote bag to create a good base for dyeing.

2 Lay your tote bag on a flat surface and iron out the creases.

3 Place your plumbing pipe diagonally across the cloth bag. Roll your bag around the pipe and secure both ends with rubber bands.

4 Wrap rubber bands around the pipe at approximately 1-inch (2.5-cm) intervals, compressing the bag as you go. Make sure they are tight enough to resist the dye, and double over if necessary. Include the handles to give an all-over finish.

5 Place the bound pipe in a soaking bucket for 30 minutes.

6 Remove the pipe from the water, squeeze out the excess water, and dab with a towel.

7 Prepare your synthetic indigo vat by filling up a tub with 4 gallons (15 L) of warm water. Sprinkle in your indigo powder and sodium hydrosulfite. Stir gently. Dissolve your soda ash in 2 tablespoons (30 ml) of hot water. Slowly add this solution to the dye vat. Leave for 30 minutes. Submerge the wrapped pipe in the dye tub and leave for 40 minutes; do not agitate as this will create bubbles.

8 Remove the pipe from the dye tub and leave to oxidize for 15 minutes. Rinse under cold water until the water runs clear. Then release the fabric from the pipe, rinse again, and wash with dishwashing liquid until the water runs clear.

## Contemporary arashi

In traditional Japanese arashi, the shibori artist uses a wooden pole instead of a plumbing pipe—as a result, this technique is often referred to as pole wrapping. Contemporary American artists were the first to use discarded plumbing pipes in shibori. The Americans also introduced bright, clashing colors and the random placement of designs on fabric, which became a well-known symbol of the Swinging Sixties.

# Mokume
# Textured stitching

Mokume is a Japanese shibori stitch technique known for its woodgrain-like textural pattern. This resist involves stitching with a needle and thread in rows of parallel running stitches. The threads are then pulled tightly, bringing the fabric together and creating gathered areas that the dye cannot penetrate. It is the most simple of the stitch resists and is a good introduction to more advanced techniques.

S titching techniques are more advanced than dip, space, or scrunch dyeing techniques. They require precision and the planning of a design. There are many different types of stitching techniques used throughout Japan that change the effect on the fabric. Often these stitches are combined on the same piece to highlight different areas and form a resist illustration. For example, mokume may be used with more advanced stitching techniques such as maki-nui and karamatsu shibori.

Despite the basic nature of mokume, there are quite a few things to remember in order to achieve the best possible result. Using a ruler and tailor's chalk allows you to map out and track where your stitches will be placed. It is also a good idea to use contrasting thread to highlight your stitched area. Experiment with small test pieces of fabric in order to understand the exact amount of tension required when pulling the threads and gathering the fabric together.

Mokume opens the door to an entire library of stitches and the possibilities that come with them. It is easy to use stitches to illustrate basic shapes, and the technique allows the artist to make more complex dyed placement prints.

3

## you will need

Iron

Cotton or natural
dyed fabric (1)

Tailor's chalk

Ruler

Sewing needle and
thread (2)

Soaking bucket

Towel

Paper mask

Rubber gloves (3)

Dye pot

Acid dye (4)

Scissors (5)

Vinegar

## Stitch ideas

Decorative stitching can also
be used to embellish finished
pieces. A Japanese craft called
sashiko traditionally goes hand in
hand with mokume.

# Using textured stitching

**1** Iron the piece of fabric, then lay it down on a hard surface.

**2** Using tailor's chalk and a ruler, draw horizontal lines on your fabric ¾ inch (2 cm) apart.

**3** Double-thread the needle and tie it off with a strong knot. Sew along the first line with running stitch. When you reach the end, cut the thread to a length of 6 inches (15 cm). Secure the end with a knot. (You will use this thread to pull all the stitches together on the line you have just sewn.)

**4** Repeat the process until all your ruled lines are stitched.

**5** Collect all the ends of thread together from each row, and gently pull then push the fabric with your other hand, creating a gathered effect. Secure the pulled threads with a tight knot.

**6** Soak the fabric in a bucket of water for 15 minutes. Remove from the water and dab the excess water with a towel.

**7** Fill the dye pot with 2½ gallons (10 L) warm water per 17 oz (500 g) of dry fabric. Prepare your acid dye by dissolving it in boiling water. Add vinegar. Place the fabric into the dye pot, ensuring it is submerged. Leave to dye in the simmering pot for 30 minutes, agitating regularly.

**8** Once the dye process is complete, rinse under warm running water, then cut the knots and remove the stitches. Rinse again until the water runs clear.

## 1 Boxes

Here, you are using a very simple, very effective, traditional technique.

Iron your fabric. Starting from the end, fold the fabric forward 2 inches (5 cm), and then fold this forward twice more (maintaining the same width) in order to create four levels of fabric that are 2 inches (5 cm), with the excess fabric coming out of the side. Iron flat. Turn your piece to the side and accordion pleat the folded fabric. Using a double-threaded needle, pass the needle through your accordion pleats in order to make the gather hold. Knot the thread to secure.

Place the fabric in a soaking bucket for 20 minutes. Prepare your synthetic indigo vat as per the instructions on page 18. Remove the bound fabric from the soaking bucket and wring out the excess water. Submerge the fabric in the dye vat and leave for 15 minutes; do not agitate.

When complete, remove from the dye vat and allow it to oxidize for 15 minutes. Rinse the fabric under cold water until the water runs clear before undoing the stitches and exposing a box pattern.

## 2 Heart

Illustrate your shibori by creating basic shapes with stitch resist.

Fold your fabric in half and iron. Using tailor's chalk, draw half a heart, using the fold as a center. Prepare a needle with double thread and knot at the end. Beginning at the top of your folded heart, follow your the line with a running stitch, gathering as you go. When you reach the end of the heart, pull the threads as tightly as possible and tie a tight knot.

Place the fabric in a soaking bucket for 10 to 15 minutes. Remember, when your fabric is wet, you may be able to tighten the stitches further due to the fabric shrinkage. Prepare your synthetic indigo vat according to the instructions on page 18. Remove your fabric from the soaking bucket and submerge the entire cloth in the dye vat for 15 minutes.

When complete, remove the fabric and allow it to oxidize for 15 minutes. Rinse under cold water until the water runs clear before undoing your stitches.

## 3 Stripes

This classic stripe design can be reinvented in so many ways—including textural.

Fold your fabric in half. Using a double-threaded needle, run the stitch along the length of your fold, gathering tightly as you go. When you reach the end, wind the thread tightly around your gathered stitched line. Then continue to wind the thread tightly down the length of the fabric for an extra 8 inches (20 cm), creating a bound tube. Spread the fabric out at this point and repeat the running stitch to form the stitched gathered line as you did originally. Wind the thread again and repeat until all fabric is bound.

Place the fabric in a soaking bucket for 20 minutes. Prepare your fiber-reactive dye according to the instructions on page 18. Remove from the soaking bucket and wring out the excess water. Submerge the fabric in the dye tub and leave for 30 minutes, agitating regularly to ensure it is dyed evenly. Remove from the dye tub and rinse under cold water until the water runs clear, and then undo the stitches.

1

2

3

# Project: Silk-stitch shibori head scarf

A great way to show off your shibori stitch skills is to transform an old silk head scarf into a beautiful accessory sure to win compliments.

When first practicing stitch shibori, it is good to start with a smaller piece and use a contrasting thread so you can see your stitches clearly. Experiment with the tension and make sure the threads are pulled tight after presoaking to ensure you get a positive result.

1 Lay your silk scarf on a flat surface and iron.

2 Starting from one end, fold the fabric forward 2 inches (5 cm) and then fold this forward twice more (maintaining the same width) in order to create four levels of fabric that are 2 inches (5 cm), with the excess fabric coming out of the side. Iron flat.

3 Turn your piece to the side by 90 degrees and accordion pleat the folded fabric. Using a double-threaded needle, sew through the accordion pleats using a running stitch in order to make the gather hold. Knot the thread to secure.

4 Soak the scarf in a bucket of water for 20 minutes. Remove from the water and dab the excess water with a towel.

5 Fill the stainless steel or enamel dye pot with warm water. Prepare the acid dye by dissolving it in just enough hot water to make a solution, and add to the dye pot. Bring the water in the dye pot to a boil. Place the scarf in the dye pot and leave for 10 minutes, agitating regularly to ensure it is evenly dyed. Add 2 tablespoons of vinegar and leave for another 20 minutes.

6 Once the dye process is complete, rinse under cold running water, then cut the knots and remove the stitches. Rinse again until the water runs clear.

## Dyeing silk

It is recommended that you use acid dye with silk to get the most intense color. While direct dyes or fiber-reactive dyes will give some color, the results will not be as vibrant as the color you anticipate. Soda ash will also have an effect on your silk and remove the sheen.

Silk habotai, also known as China silk, is a lightweight silk commonly used for scarves. It has a plain weave and is often used by artists to paint on and embellish. It is sturdy enough to manipulate with stitches and has a beautiful luster, so it would work well with this technique.

Cotton voile is a good alternative to silk. It has similar properties and dyes well with fiber-reactive dye, indigo, or direct dyes.

# Kumo Spider-web binding

"Kumo"—meaning spider in Japanese—
creates patterns that resemble the fine lines
of a spider's web. This technique can be
realized in many surprising and unexpected
ways, the most popular being the tie-dye
or hippie circles that made these dyeing
techniques household patterns.

Kumo is made up of a series of circles placed within one
another, from large to small, that seem to be joined
together by the imprints of the bind lines. The basic
principle of kumo is to pull a peak in the fabric and bind fine
thread from the bottom of the area that has been peaked, to the
top, and back down to the bottom. This creates a sausage shape
of bound fabric. At its base, the rest of the fabric spreads out and
the process is repeated, depending on how many web-like
patterns you wish to see on the final piece. The pattern can be
transformed by altering the size of each bound circle or varying
the spacing between the binding.

Traditionally, a hook or similar tool is used to create the peak so
that both hands are free to bind. In order to make the binding
process easier for beginners, it is a good idea to insert a
toothpick or similar object into the peak in order to hold it in
place and create a firm base on which to bind.

Kumo works especially well on a silk dupioni or similar silk with
a tight weave. The natural slub found in silk adds extra spider-
like textures, and the tightly woven fibers emphasize the delicate
lines of the web. This technique is commonly seen detailing
vintage kimonos, and is one of the more recognizable Japanese
shibori techniques.

## you will need

Iron

Piece of white or lightly colored silk (1)

Toothpicks (2)

Polyester or nylon thread (3)

Small scissors (4)

Soaking bucket

Towel

Paper mask

Rubber gloves (5)

Dye tub

Wooden spoon (6)

Acid dye (7)

# How to bind and dye a spider-web pattern

**1** Iron your piece of silk.

**2** Create a peak by positioning a toothpick underneath the fabric.

**3** Wrap the fabric around the toothpick to create little pleats.

**4** Holding the base of the toothpick and the thread, bind the thread from the base of the peak to the top and back down. Secure the thread with a knot and cut the end.

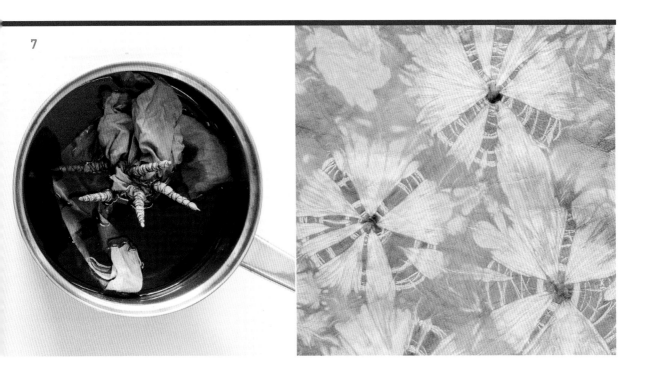

**5** Repeat until you have a cluster of bound toothpicks.

**6** Soak the fabric in a bucket of water for 20 minutes. Remove the fabric from the water and dab the excess water with a towel.

**7** Prepare your fiber-reactive dye by dissolving it in just enough warm water to make a solution. Boil 4 pints (2 L) of water and add your dye solution to it. Place the fabric in the dye, ensuring that it is submerged. Leave for 30 minutes, agitating regularly.

**8** Rinse under cold running water, remove the binding and toothpicks from the fabric, and rinse the fabric again until the water runs clear.

## 1 Heat set

The beautiful peaks of heat-set kumo add an incredible tactile element to cloth.

This technique is often used on silk; however, washing will destroy the kumo impressions. To avoid this, use heat-set synthetic fabric that will maintain its shape after washing. Dampen the synthetic fabric with a spray bottle of water. Create a small peak from the underside of the fabric. Pinch the top of this peak and bind from the base to the top and back down again with thread, tying off securely. Repeat until you reach the desired number of peaks.

Wrap the bound piece in newspaper or cheesecloth to protect it. Place in your bamboo steamer. Fill your wok with a little boiling water, place the bamboo steamer in the wok, and steam for 20 minutes. When cooled, remove the fabric from the steamer, unwrap it, and test by undoing a bound peak. If you are happy with the heat-set piece, continue to remove the thread. If your fabric is thick or very large, it may require another 10 minutes of steaming. Re-bind the test peak and continue to steam. Your piece is now finished, and washing in cold water is optional.

## 2 Large

Playing with scale highlights the delicate webbed lines of kumo.

Lay your fabric on a flat surface. Using your thumb and index finger, pinch the center of your fabric to the desired size of your kumo circle. Place a rubber band at the base to secure. Dampen your gathered circle to just above the rubber band. Using synthetic thread, wind from the base of the circle to the tip and back down again, then tie off.

Place the fabric in a soaking bucket for 10 minutes. Prepare your synthetic indigo vat as per the instructions on page 18. Remove the fabric from the soaking bucket and wring out the excess water. Holding the fabric securely at the base of the rubber band, submerge the entire gathered circle in your dye tub for 10 minutes (you may have to hold it or drape it over the side).

Remove the fabric and be careful not to splash the white areas and allow it to oxidize for 15 minutes. Rinse with cold water running away from the white section until the water runs clear.

## 3 Two color dyes

This creates delicate kumo circles on a hand-dyed block color background.

Lay your fabric flat and pinch the fabric to the desired size of your circle. Place a rubber band at the base. Dampen your gathered circle to just above the rubber band. Using synthetic thread, wind from the base to the tip and back down again, then tie off. Bind more circles as desired.

Soak your fabric for 10 minutes. Prepare your synthetic indigo vat as per the instructions on page 18. Remove the fabric from the soaking bucket and wring out the excess water. Holding the fabric securely at the base of all the rubber bands, submerge only the gathered circles in your dye vat for 10 minutes.

Remove your fabric from the dye vat and allow it to oxidize for 15 minutes. Rinse with cold water running away from the white section. Cover your rinsed peaks with plastic food wrap (this will protect them from the second dye) and secure with rubber bands. Prepare your fiber-reactive dye as per the instructions on page 18. Add the bound piece for 30 minutes. Remove, rinse, unbind, and rinse again until the water runs clear.

# Project: Kumo duvet cover and pillowcases

A great project to decorate your bedroom or give old bedding a new lease on life. Kumo can be used in different sizes and repeats to create a unique bedding collection.

This project involves indigo dye but would also work with a fiber-reactive or direct dye.

1 Lay out your white or lightly colored cotton duvet cover, right-side up. Find the center of your duvet cover and lift up to the desired size of your kumo circle. Place a rubber band at the base to secure.

2 Wet the gathered area to just above the rubber band. Using synthetic thread, wind tightly from the base of the circle to the tip and back down again, forming a large gathered circle. Secure the thread with a knot and cut the end.

3 Soak the gathered circle in a bucket of water for 20 minutes.

4 Prepare your synthetic indigo vat by filling up a tub with 4 gallons (15 L) of warm water. Sprinkle in your indigo powder and sodium hydrosulfite. Stir gently. Dissolve your soda ash in 2 tablespoons (30 ml) of hot water. Slowly add this solution to the dye vat. Leave for 15 minutes.

5 Remove the fabric from the water and dab the excess water with a towel. Holding the fabric securely at the base of the rubber band, submerge the entire gathered circle in the dye tub for 10 minutes (you may have to hold it or drape it over the side).

6 Remove and be careful not to mark the white areas with dye. Rinse with cold water running away from the white section until the water runs clear. Undo the binding and wash with dishwashing liquid and cold water.

## Contemporary kumo

To complement your duvet cover, you can create some mismatched kumo pillowcases. Experiment with mapping out your kumo circles, clusters of kumo circles, and random scattered circles.

When using indigo for bedding, it is recommended that you soak the piece in a bucket of boiling water after dyeing. This removes any excess dye particles and prevents dye transfer.

Never wash indigo-dyed pieces with laundry detergent; always use dishwashing liquid.

# Heat-setting fabric

Often the beauty of shibori is in the binding and its three-dimensional state. It is sometimes difficult to imagine undoing all your intricate bindings, since the sculptural form can be just as amazing as the finished cloth. While you can also dye heat-set fabrics, this technique emphasizes the sculptural aspect of this age-old craft.

To heat-set fabric, 100% polyester fabric is bound, as if it is about to be put in a dye vat. Instead, the material is subjected to heat, in a receptacle such as a steamer or pressure cooker. This sets the binding in place and maintains the beautiful sculptural qualities that are lost when the focus is on the dyeing, and the binding is unwrapped and fabric ironed.

Polyester is a thermoplastic material, meaning that when heat is applied, the fibers meld and fix into place. Silk can also be used for this technique by boiling or steaming the fabric, and then allowing the piece to dry in the bound form. However, the effects are not as permanent, and items should be dry cleaned to prevent them from losing their shape.

Several artists focus on this technique, exploring the form created by shibori rather than on the two-dimensional pattern created by the dye. The use of heat-set shibori is commonly found on scarves and couture blouses where the fashion designer uses the relief qualities as a feature for his/her piece.

1

5

3

# you will need

Tailor's chalk (1)

Ruler (2)

Piece of 100% polyester fabric (3)

Marbles (4)

Rubber bands (5)

Newspaper or cheesecloth (6)

Old bamboo steamer (7)

Old wok

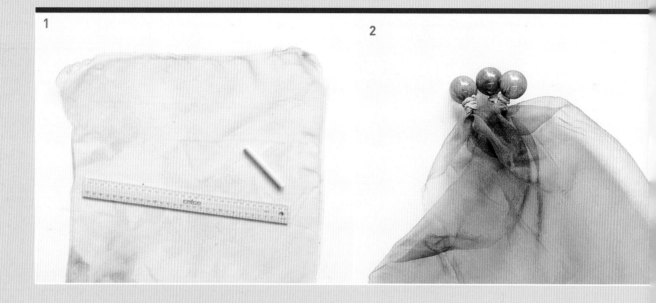

# How to heat-set your fabric

**1** Using tailor's chalk and a ruler, mark the area you wish to bind. (This is not essential, since you may wish to randomly scatter or cluster your design.)

**2** Following the marked-out areas, place a marble on the underside of the cloth and bind with a rubber band.

**3** Repeat until you have bound all your marked areas. Be sure to keep them all on the same side of the cloth because this will affect the shape of the overall piece.

**4** Wrap the bound piece in newspaper or cheesecloth to protect it.

**5** Place the piece in your bamboo steamer. Sit the steamer in the wok and fill with enough boiling water to cover the base of the steamer but not touch the piece. Steam the piece for 20 minutes. Keep an eye on the water level—you may need to add more water to prevent the wok from boiling dry.

**6** Remove the steamer from the wok, allow the piece to cool, then remove it from the steamer.

**7** Unwrap the piece from the newspaper and remove a marble to test the shape of the fabric. If you are happy with the heat-set piece, continue to remove the bands. If your fabric is thick or very large, it may require another 10 minutes of steaming. If this is the case, re-band the test marble and continue to steam.

**8** Your piece is now finished and may be washed in cold water, if desired.

# 1 Star

Every shibori technique can be converted into a heat-set variation because all processes include aspects of three-dimensional sculpture—retaining this shape can often be very simple!

Use a steam iron and 100% synthetic organza. Pleat the fabric horizontally with folds of approximately 4 inches (10 cm) and steam these accordion pleats into your fabric. Instead of folding your fabric vertically into a square shape, try to replicate a triangle shape. Fold your fabric back and forth following the line of a triangle shape, much like making samosas! This will produce a pleated triangle stack (see page 22 for diagram). Re-press and steam. When the fabric has cooled, open the fabric to reveal your structural piece.

# 2 Arashi

The compression used to create arashi is an ideal texture to create a beautiful sculptural piece.

Use 100% synthetic organza or similar fabric. Find a small metal pole or similar (even an old can). Do not use a regular plumbing pipe because it will melt if placed in a steamer. Roll the synthetic strip of fabric around your pole or can. Secure both ends with rubber bands. Stand the wrapped pole upright on the table. Place rubber bands at approximately ½-inch (1-cm) intervals down the pole. Push the fabric down hard, compressing the cloth between the bands. This compression is what creates your pleat-like textures. Place in a large bamboo steamer and steam for 20 minutes. Remove, allow to cool, and then unbind to reveal the structural piece.

# 3 Different-sized marbles

An effective way to modify the scale of heat-set molding is to use different-sized resists.

Randomly select areas to band your small and larger marbles. Be sure to keep them all on the same side of the cloth, as this will affect the overall piece. Continue until you have bound all the fabric.

Wrap the bound piece in newspaper or cheesecloth to protect it. Place in your bamboo steamer. Fill your wok with a little boiling water, place the bamboo steamer in the wok, and steam for 20 minutes. When cooled, remove the fabric from the steamer, unwrap it, and test by removing a marble. If you are happy with the heat-set piece, continue to remove the bands. If your fabric is thick or very large, it may require another 10 minutes of steaming. Re-band the test marble and continue to steam.

Your piece is now finished, and may be washed in cold water, if desired.

# Project: High-fashion heat-set scarf

Fine heat-set pleats create a beautiful, intricate scarf that is worthy of a feature in any fashion runway show or magazine.

When practicing heat-set shibori, remember that synthetics are thermoplastic materials and get very hot.

1 Lay a sheet of plastic food wrap on a flat surface. Place your 100% synthetic organza of the same size on top.

2 Pleat the fabric horizontally with approximately ½-inch (1-cm) accordion pleats, using the plastic food wrap to hold the pleats in place.

3 Continue along the length of the fabric.

4 Carefully clamp each end of your pleated fabric and wrap, holding the pleats firmly together.

5 Place the piece in your bamboo steamer. Sit the steamer in the wok and fill with enough boiling water to cover the base of the steamer but not touch the piece. Steam the piece for 20 minutes. Keep an eye on the water level—you may need to add more water to prevent the wok from boiling dry.

6 Remove the steamer from the wok, allow the piece to cool, then remove it from the steamer.

7 When the fabric has cooled, open the pleats and remove the wrap to reveal your heat-set pleated scarf. Your piece is now finished and may be washed in cold water, if desired.

## Heat-setting and fabrics

This technique can also be done using silk or cotton fabric; however, in order to maintain your pleats, it would be a dry-clean-only item, as washing would remove the pleats, returning the fabric to its previous state.

Many fashion designers have used this technique in their collections, with Japanese fashion icon Issey Miyake being one of the first to bring this to the world's attention.

# Pleating stripes

Stripes are a classic design found in many industries, and in many different styles. The notion of creating a handmade stripe, reflecting the decisions that the creator has made, makes shibori stripes very special.

While it is possible to create stripes using other techniques such as arashi (see page 36) and shape resists (see page 76), the most basic process can be the most satisfying. This stripe technique follows a similar process to a shape resist, but without the shape. The folding techniques are used to create the stripe, and the clamps are used to hold it in place, but the effect is achieved by simply dipping half the pleated fabric into the dye.

This technique has a strong design element because you can largely determine your final product before beginning. It is therefore important to plan your stripes. They can be altered through the size of the fold, the areas that are dipped, the angle of the pleats, and whether other techniques are included, such as double stitching.

Stripe techniques are very easy to do, and adding these layers can make the process and design more complex based on the artist's comfort levels, curiosity, and aesthetic desires. Stripes can be all different widths, two-tone or multicolored, ombré, strong or tonal, or bleeding. There are so many variations within this simple technique. It is a great place to start, and you are sure to achieve professional results, even as a beginner. Stripes are timeless, and shibori allows you to make yours personal.

# you will need

Iron

Piece of white or lightly colored cotton (1)

Tailor's chalk (2)

Ruler (3)

Pegs or clamps (4)

Soaking bucket

Towel

Shallow dye tub wide enough to accommodate the length of the stripe (5)

Paper mask

Rubber gloves (6)

Fiber-reactive dye (7)

# Creating dyed stripes

**1** Iron the piece of fabric, then lay it down on a hard surface.

**2** Using tailor's chalk and a ruler, draw horizontal lines on your fabric 4 inches (10 cm) apart.

**3** Accordion pleat the ruled lines by folding the fabric one way and then the other, ironing each pleat into place.

**4** Secure the pleats together with clamps.

4

6

**5** Soak the fabric in a bucket of water for 10 minutes. Remove from the water and dab the excess water with a towel.

**6** Prepare your fiber-reactive dye by dissolving it in just enough warm water to make a solution, and add it to a shallow tub containing 2 pints (1 L) of water. Dissolve salt and soda ash separately in hot water and add to the tub (see fiber-reactive recipe on page 18 for guidance on amounts). Holding the clamps, drape the edge of the pleats into the shallow dye tub. The stripe will be double the level dipped when it is unfolded. Leave for 30 minutes.

**7** Once the dye process is complete, carefully remove the fabric, making sure you do not mark the white area with the dye.

**8** Rinse under cold running water, then remove the clamps. Rinse again until the water runs clear.

## 1 Two color dyes

Stripes in two colors look very effective.

Iron your fabric. Rule lines on your fabric with tailor's chalk at 4-inch (10-cm) intervals, accordion pleat these lines, and iron into place. Secure with clamps.

Place the fabric in a soaking bucket for 10 minutes. Prepare your fiber-reactive dye according to the instructions on page 18. Remove your piece from the soaking bucket and wipe off the excess water with a towel. Holding the clamps, drape the edge of your pleats in the shallow dye tub (remember, the stripe will be double the level dipped when it is unfolded). Leave for 30 minutes.

Carefully remove the fabric, making sure you do not get the white area in the dye. Holding the clamps, rinse the dyed area under cold water. Then swap the clamps to the side that has just been dyed. Prepare the second dye color according to the instructions and repeat the process, draping the white side of the fabric into the second dye tub and leaving for 15 minutes. Then remove, rinse under cold water, undo the clamps, and rinse again until the water runs clear.

## 2 Over-dyed

This technique allows you to add to a colored fabric you already love.

Start with a colored fabric of a light tone. Lay your fabric flat and iron. Using a ruler and tailor's chalk, rule lines on your fabric at 4-inch (10-cm) intervals, accordion pleat these lines, and iron into place. Secure with clamps.

Place the fabric in a soaking bucket for 10 minutes. Prepare your fiber-reactive dye by dissolving it in a small amount of warm water and then add to a pot containing 4 pints (2 L) of water. Dissolve salt and soda ash in hot water and add it to the pot. Pour into a dye tub. Remove your piece from the soaking bucket and wipe off the excess water with a towel. Holding the clamps, drape the edge of your pleats into the shallow dye tub (remember, the stripe will be double the level dipped when it is unfolded) and leave for 30 minutes.

Once the dye process is complete, carefully remove the fabric, making sure you do not get the white area in the dye. Rinse under cold water, undo the clamps, and rinse again until the water runs clear.

## 3 Bound

This is a super-easy example of how to produce abstract stripes with lots of texture.

Lay the fabric on a flat surface. Using both hands at either end of the fabric, gather it together as if you were creating small, messy accordion pleats, then bind extremely tightly with rubber bands at 3-inch (7.5-cm) intervals.

Place the fabric in a soaking bucket for 10 minutes. Prepare your fiber-reactive dye by dissolving it in a small amount of warm water. Then add it to a pot containing 4 pints (2 L) of water. Dissolve salt and soda ash in hot water and add it to the pot.

Submerge your bound piece and leave for 30 minutes. Then remove, rinse under cold water, unbind, and rinse again until the water runs clear. Notice how you have stronger lines where your resist was, and softer ones where the fabric was scrunched.

# Project: Striped sarong

Step away from the basic straight stripe and add a bit of fun with this quirky, hot-pink diamond version. It only takes an extra fold or two to take this sarong from a strip of cotton to a vacation in the Maldives.

The beauty of stripes is that their simplicity is timeless.

1 Fold the white or lightly colored sarong in half horizontally and in half again vertically.

2 Beginning from the folded center corner, iron 4-inch (10-cm) accordion pleats on a 45-degree angle until you are left with a fully pleated strip.

3 Secure one side of the strip with clamps to hold the pleats, and soak the fabric in a bucket of water for 10 minutes. Remove from the water and dab the excess water with a towel.

4 Prepare your fiber-reactive dye by dissolving it in just enough warm water to make a solution. Add it to a pot filled with 4 pints (2 L) of water. Dissolve salt and soda ash separately in hot water and add to pot (see fiber-reactive recipe on page 18 for guidance on amounts).

5 Pour 2½ inches (6 cm) of dye solution into a shallow dye tub large enough to accommodate the length of the pleated strip.

6 Holding your clamps, carefully place one side of the pleated strip into the dye and leave for 1 hour.

7 Carefully remove from the dye, making sure you do not mark the white area with the dye, and rinse with cold water running away from the white side. Undo the clamps and rinse again until the water runs clear.

## Pleats and presoaking

When using the pleated stripes technique, it is advised that you check between the pleats while dyeing to make sure the dye is penetrating between the folds. If an item has not been soaked correctly beforehand, areas will remain dry and this will cause uneven stripes.

Presoaking is a vital step in the dyeing process as it aids in the even spread of your dye and avoids blotchy marks. Since fabric shrinks when it is wet, presoaking your bound pieces is recommended as it allows you to check the tension of your resist. If your bindings are loose, it is better to find out at this stage than when the dyeing process is complete.

4

# Itajime
## Shape resist

Itajime is a shape resist technique. It is one of the most exciting and versatile tie-dye/shibori techniques. By folding fabric and clamping shapes into place, you can create patterns as basic or as intricate as you desire.

Shape-resist shibori uses two flat shapes sandwiched together to form a resist on the fabric. These shapes need to be held securely with either clamps, rubber bands, or twine. The device you choose to use to hold the shapes will determine the effect you get between the shape pattern. Using clamps will leave a clean space between your shapes, but using bands or twine will form another resist leaving fine lines, giving additional texture to your piece.

The beauty of Itajime is that you, the creator, are given the option to plan your design. Depending on the desired result, you can design a piece that is very structured and geometric with fine lines, or a loosely folded artistic piece with lots of soft bleeding dye textures. It is important that the artist considers the fabric choice when using the shape resist technique; if the fabric is too thick, the resist will not be secure enough to prevent the dye from penetrating.

Itajime shibori relies on an accordion fold whereby the fabric is folded back and forth, resembling an accordion. This fold ensures that the fabric is always on the outside rather than being folded upon itself, making sure the dye can evenly penetrate. This fold also provides a pattern, and the size of your pleats will determine the spacing between your shape pattern.

5

## you will need

Rubber gloves (1)

Paper mask

Spoon (2)

Fiber-reactive dye (3)

Dye tub

Iron

White or lightly
colored natural
fiber cloth (4)

Two matching resist
shapes (5)

Clamps, rubber
bands, or twine (6)

Soaking bucket

Tongs for removing
your fabric from
dye (7)

Dishwashing liquid

Salt

Soda ash

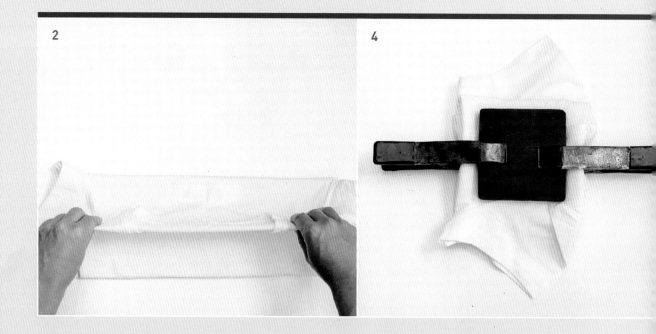

# How to tie-dye using shape resists

**1** Iron your fabric. In this example, we use a cotton T-shirt (see also the T-shirt project on pages 82–83).

**2** Begin pleating your fabric horizontally. The size of your pleat is determined by the size of your resist shape and hence the spacing of your geometric pattern.

**3** You now need to repeat this fold on the vertical to create a square shape.

**4** Place your fabric between your two matching shapes, and ensure your shapes are perfectly lined up, creating a resist. Secure the shapes in place with your clamps, twine, or rubber bands.

**5** Leave to soak in a bucket of water for several minutes, ensuring the fabric is completely wet. This fills the fibers of your fabric, which means you will get a more even dye result and the dye is less likely to rush in and penetrate your resist.

NOTE: It is a good idea to ensure your clamps and bands are tight enough at this point, as fabric shrinks when wet.

**6** Prepare your fiber-reactive dye by dissolving it in just enough warm water to make a solution, and add it to a pot containing 4 pints (2 L) of water. Dissolve salt and soda ash separately in hot water and add to the pot (see fiber-reactive recipe on page 18 for guidance on amounts). Place your wet fabric item into your dye pot, making sure the item is fully immersed.

**7** Leave for 15 minutes, stirring occasionally.

# 1 Pegging

This is a modern-day version of shape resist, as it is highly effective and simple to do using household clothespins. Here is a piece of lightweight cotton dyed using indigo dye.

Pleat your fabric horizontally with folds of approximately 4 inches (10 cm). Re-pleat vertically, with folds of approximately 4 inches (10 cm) to create a square shape. Place as many clothespins on the two sides of the square as you wish. We love the look of just a few; it is simple, elegant, and very Japanese inspired.

Soak in warm water for 5 minutes. Prepare your synthetic indigo dye vat according to the instructions on page 18. Gently place your fabric in your indigo vat. Leave for 15 minutes without agitating. Remove and allow to sit to oxidize for 15 minutes.

Rinse thoroughly before taking off your clothespins. Rinse any residual dye, remove the clothespins, and unfold. Wash with dishwashing liquid.

# 2 Circles

Circle shape resist can be done using craft shapes or simple jar lids.

The size of your pleat is determined by the size of your resist shape and hence the spacing of your geometric pattern. This example uses a 4¾-inch (12-cm) deep pleat and 4-inch (10-cm) jar lids on 20 inches (50 cm) of lightweight cotton.

Begin pleating your fabric horizontally. You now need to re-pleat this fold on the vertical to create a square shape. Place your fabric between your matching 4-inch (10-cm) jar lids, secure with clamps, and soak in warm water for 5 minutes. Prepare your synthetic indigo dye vat according to the instructions on page 18. Gently place your fabric in your indigo vat. Leave for 15 minutes without agitating. Remove and allow to sit to oxidize for 15 minutes.

Rinse thoroughly before taking off your circle resist. Rinse any residual dye, remove the lids, and unfold. Wash with dishwashing liquid.

# 3 Triangles

This triangular geometric pattern is really popular and fun to do. You'll need two flat triangle shapes to create the resist.

Pleat the fabric horizontally, with folds of approximately 4 inches (10 cm), then instead of folding your fabric vertically into a square shape, you must replicate the triangle shapes being used as a resist. Fold your fabric back and forth following the line of your triangle shape, much like making samosas! See page 22 for diagrams.

Place your fabric between your matching 4-inch (10-cm) triangle shapes, secure with clamps, and soak in warm water for 5 minutes. Prepare your synthetic indigo dye vat according to the instructions on page 18. Gently place your fabric in your indigo vat. Leave for 15 minutes without agitating. Remove and allow to sit to oxidize for 15 minutes.

Rinse thoroughly before taking off your triangle resist. Rinse any residual dye, remove shapes, and unfold. Wash with dishwashing liquid.

# Project: Windowpane T-shirt

This T-shirt was dyed using indigo dye, which is very good for shape resist because it is a surface dye (it sits on the surface of the fiber) and creates some great tones and textures.

The sleeves of the T-shirt are left out of the fold in order for them to remain solid blue. Since a T-shirt has a front and a back and is quite thick, large squares are used for the resist in order to keep folding to a minimum.

1 Pleat your T-shirt horizontally, with folds of approximately 5½ inches (14 cm).

2 You now need to re-pleat this fold on the vertical to create a square shape; again, the pleat fold is 5½ inches (14 cm) deep.

3 Place your T-shirt between your matching 4¾-inch (12-cm) squares and secure with clamps, leaving the sleeves out.

4 Prepare your synthetic indigo dye vat as per the instructions on page 18. Place the T-shirt in the vat and leave for 15 minutes.

5 Remove and allow to oxidize for 15 minutes.

6 Rinse thoroughly before taking off your square resists. Rinse any residual dye, remove the square resists, and unfold.

7 Wash with dishwashing liquid and rinse until the water runs clear. Hang on the line to dry.

## Indigo dye

Indigo dye is a natural dye used all over the world that is well known for its distinctive blue color. It is most commonly used for the dyeing of denim jeans. Indigo dye belongs to the dye family known as vat dyes. It is not soluble in water; to be dissolved, it must undergo a chemical change. Your dyed item is always green when first removed from your indigo vat. After several minutes of being exposed to air, the dyed fabric changes from green to blue. This is known as oxidizing (reacting with the oxygen in the air). While making an indigo vat is more work than many of the other commercial dyes available, it is well worth the effort because the results are unique and the process is fascinating. Items dyed with indigo should always be washed with dishwashing liquid to prevent dye transfer.

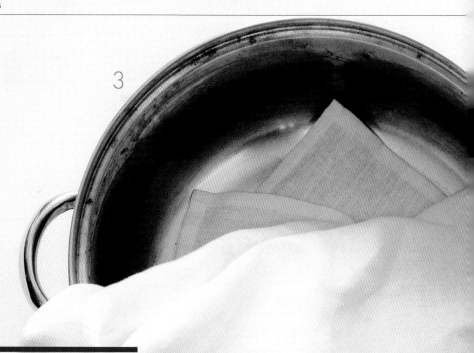

# Scrunch

The simplest technique is often the most effective. With scrunch, fabric is gathered or scrunched randomly and bound with twine or rubber bands before being dyed. The pattern is random and abstract, with directional branch-like lines revealing themselves throughout the fabric.

The tension of the binding in scrunch dyeing determines the amount of pattern or texture on the piece. If it is too tight, no color can seep in, leaving very little pattern. If it is too loose, the dye will penetrate through, leaving very little texture. The tension of the bands or twine will inform the design and leave a delicate imprint of the binding resist.

The beauty of the technique is that you can choose to plunge into the unknown, scrunching and binding at random and then unwrapping an intricate surprise at the end. At the other end of the spectrum, as you master the technique, you can direct your design and start to influence the results.

Scrunch dyeing has a strong fashion application because it can be easily used with unusually shaped garments, which may be difficult to pleat or fold. The aesthetic can be very soft and

subtle, or strong and striking. If you aren't happy with your results, you can rescrunch. Start soft and then add layers if you're not sure what you want. However, the unexpected results may provide what you never knew you were after. Always remember: it may not be until you are ironing the dry fabric that the beauty of shibori is revealed.

Scrunch can be one color or multicolored. If you are using a fiber-reactive dye, you may want to utilize some of the space dyeing techniques on pages 108–113. Pouring color into different sections of your scrunch gives bursts of random color, and when done subtly, it makes an interesting feature piece. Indigo is highly effective with this technique, since it gives many different levels of tone that add to the random pattern.

2

4

---

## you will need

Cotton or natural
fiber fabric (1)

Rubber bands or
twine (2)

Soaking bucket

Towel

Paper mask

Rubber gloves

Dye tub (3)

Fiber-reactive dye (4)

Salt

Soda ash

# How to scrunch dye

**1** Gather your fabric and bunch it together in a random fashion.

**2** Secure each scrunch with rubber bands or twine.

**3** Soak the fabric in a bucket of water for 15 minutes. Remove from the water and dab the excess water with a towel.

**4** Check your bands or twine are tight enough to resist the dye; when the cloth is wet, it shrinks.

**3**

**5**

**5** Fill the dye tub with
4 gallons (15 L) warm water
per 17 oz (500g) dry fabric.
Prepare your fiber-reactive
dye by dissolving it in a
small amount of warm water
and then add it to a pot.
Dissolve salt and soda ash in
hot water and add to the pot.

**6** Leave for approximately
20 minutes.

**7** Once the dye process is
complete, remove the fabric
from the dye tub, rinse
under cold running water,
and then remove the
binding. Rinse again until
the water runs clear.

## 1 Twice dyed

Using two colors with this technique creates depth and a variety of hues.

Gather your fabric randomly and bunch it together. Secure it with rubber bands or twine. Place the fabric in a soaking bucket for 15 minutes. Remove your piece from the soaking bucket, wipe off the excess water with a towel, and check that your bands or twine are tight enough to resist the dye, in case of fabric shrinkage.

Fill your dye tub with 4 pints (2 L) of water per 17 oz (100g) of dry fabric. Prepare the lighter-colored dye by dissolving it in a small amount of boiling water, then pour it into the dye tub. Dissolve salt and soda ash in hot water and add to the tub. Submerge your fabric in the dye tub for approximately 20 minutes. Rinse the bound piece under cold water with the resists still intact. Undo the fabric, rescrunch, and secure again with bands or twine. Mix up the darker-colored dye as you did the lighter one and add it to a second dye tub. Dissolve soda ash and salt and add to the pot. Add the bound piece and leave for 15 minutes.

Then remove, unbind, and rinse under cold water until the water runs clear.

## 2 Scrunch with indigo dye

The scrunch technique allows indigo to truly express itself in its form as a stunning surface pattern.

Gather your fabric randomly and bunch it together. Secure with bands or twine. Place the fabric in a soaking bucket for 15 minutes. Remove your piece from the soaking bucket, wipe off the excess water with a towel and check that your bands or twine are tight enough to resist the dye, in case of fabric shrinkage. If you can get your fingers under the twine or bands, they are not tight enough to resist the dye.

Prepare the synthetic indigo vat according to the instructions on page 18. Submerge your fabric in the dye tub for approximately 15 minutes. Remove the fabric and allow to oxidize for 15 minutes.

Rinse the bound piece under cold water until the water runs clear, then unbind and rinse again.

## 3 Placement scrunch

Using the scrunch technique in just a selected area can add dramatic effect to a garment.

Select an area on your cloth or premade clothing item. Gather your fabric randomly and bunch it together. Secure with bands or twine. Place the fabric in a soaking bucket for 15 minutes. If you wish to keep the unbound area white, or the original fabric color, it is a good idea to protect it with a plastic bag that can hang outside the dye tub.

Fill your dye tub with 4 pints (2 L) of water per 17 oz (100g) of dry fabric. Prepare the dye by dissolving it in a small amount of boiling water, then pour it into the dye tub. Dissolve salt and soda ash in hot water and add to the pot. Remove your piece from the soaking bucket and wipe off the excess water with a towel. Submerge your fabric in the dye tub for approximately 30 minutes.

Remove and rinse the bound piece under cold water until the water runs clear, then unbind and rinse again.

# Project: Boutique indigo tablecloth

Stunning textures, and beautiful tones and lines can be achieved on large-scale pieces to make a tablecloth perfect for entertaining. Two levels of scrunch give depth by adding layers of tone to the piece using different shades of the same dye.

It is important to always check the tightness of your rubber bands or twine; if it is too loose, too much dye will penetrate through and your scrunch will lack definition.

1 Gather and scrunch areas of your table cloth and secure tightly with rubber bands or twine. Leave enough room to include further scrunches of a second level or shade.

2 Soak your bound tablecloth in a soaking bucket for 40 minutes.

3 Prepare your synthetic indigo dye vat according to the instructions on page 18.

4 Remove your bound tablecloth from the soaking bucket, wipe off excess water with a towel, and carefully lower it into your indigo vat. Leave for 15 minutes, without agitating.

5 Carefully remove the tablecloth from the indigo vat and allow to oxidize in a bucket for 15 minutes. Your tablecloth will now turn from green to blue.

6 Rinse the tablecloth under water without removing the bindings. Re-scrunch the extra cloth around your bound areas. Add more bands to tightly secure. Your tablecloth should now be very small and tightly bound.

7 Place back into the indigo dye tub. Leave for 15 minutes. Remove and leave to oxidize in a bucket for 15 minutes.

8 Rinse the bound piece under cold water until the water runs clear. Unbind, rinse again, and wash with dishwashing liquid.

## Scrunch tips

The scrunch technique is a great technique to use for larger, bulkier items, as it does not require intricate pleats or stitches.

Indigo is a surface dye and works with layers of color. It is said that the optimum darkness is achieved after 20 minutes in the dye tub; however, removing the piece and allowing it to oxidize before returning it to the tub again builds layers of color, adding darker shades.

While this two-tone scrunch technique works well with all colors, it looks particularly striking with a neutral color scheme such as black and gray.

# Yanagi
## Willow tree patterns

"Yanagi" is Japanese for willow. The delicate lines resemble the lines of the willow trees often seen in Japan. Yanagi is a technique that uses two distinct resists simultaneously —pleating and rope—to produce a collaboration of pattern.

3

4

In the yanagi technique, the cloth is pleated in knife pleats before being bound around a thick rope and secured with twine. The overwhelming appearance can be a tonal patchwork or boxed where the lines of twine and rope meet, but on closer inspection, these resists are soft with subtle discrepancies, movement, and the exposure of bind lines.

The knife pleat is the most common sewing pleat. It is a single pleat turned in one direction, like steps. This pleat is used in yanagi because it protects one layer, which is underneath, and exposes another layer. The fabric is then bound around a rope because it provides a flexible base that can be manipulated in order to fit into a dye tub. The rope can also be rolled around itself in a snail-like manner, adding another level of texture. Twine is used to secure the cloth along the rope at regular intervals or with random spacing, depending on your individual style. The thickness of your twine will also impact your finished result, leaving heavy and thick resist lines or fine and delicate lines in its path.

This is a more advanced technique for people who are patient and precise, and want to see the labors of their work in the detail of their fabric. The freedom is left to the artist to decide the best materials, pleat sizes, and pleat styles, as well as twine size, binding technique, dye colors, and color placement. By changing these variables, yanagi can continue to surprise the creator.

## you will need

Iron

Cotton or natural fiber fabric, approximately 12 x 20 inches (30 x 50 cm) (1)

*NOTE:* The size of your fabric is determined by the size of your rope. Ideally, your pleated fabric will fit around the rope without overlapping to avoid ghosting or masked-out patterns.

21½ inches (55 cm) of thick rope, approximately 1¾ inches (4.5 cm) diameter (2)

Rubber bands

Synthetic thread (3)

Soaking bucket

Paper mask

Rubber gloves (4)

Towel

Dye tub

Fiber-reactive dye (5)

Salt

Soda ash

# How to achieve
# yanagi patterning

**1** Iron the piece of fabric, then lay it down on a hard surface.

**2** Iron ½-inch (1-cm) pleats into your fabric. It is very important that your pleats are all in one direction. You may choose to mark out your pleat intervals with tailor's chalk; however, the organic nature of this design lends itself to uneven pleats.

**3** Lay your fabric along the length of the rope.

**4** Secure the ends of the pleated fabric to either end of the rope with rubber bands.

**5** Tie the synthetic thread securely to one end of the rope. Wind the thread firmly around the fabric-covered rope at random intervals. Continue down the length of the rope, tying it securely at the bottom.

**6** Soak the fabric in a bucket of water for 15 minutes. Remove from the water and dab the excess water with a towel.

**7** Prepare your fiber-reactive dye by dissolving it in just enough warm water to create a solution, and add it to a pot containing 4 pints (2 L) of water. Dissolve salt and soda ash separately in hot water and add to the pot (see fiber-reactive recipe on page 18 for guidance on amounts). Leave for a maximum of 30 minutes, agitating regularly.

**8** Once the dye process is complete, remove the fabric from the dye tub, rinse under cold running water, and then remove the binding. Rinse again until the water runs clear.

## 1 Honeycomb

This pattern is beautiful, unexpected, simple, effective, and as delicious as a honeycomb itself.

Lay your fabric on a flat surface. Place a piece of string horizontally across the bottom and ensure it extends 1 inch (2.5 cm) longer than the fabric on each side. Loosely roll your fabric over the string so that your fabric forms a loose sleeve with the string in the middle. Tie the two ends of the string together in a tight knot. This method will cause the material to gather and scrunch.

Place your scrunchie-like piece in a soaking bucket for 20 minutes. Prepare the synthetic indigo vat according to the instructions on page 18. Remove your piece from the soaking bucket and wipe off the excess water with a towel. Submerge your fabric in the dye vat for approximately 15 minutes.

Remove the fabric and allow it to oxidize for 15 minutes. Rinse the bound piece under cold water until the water runs clear, before unbinding and rinsing again.

## 2 Diagonal

Play with the elements of design; this is classic yanagi in a different direction.

Lay your fabric on a flat surface and iron out any creases. Iron ½-inch (1-cm) knife pleats into your fabric. Wrap your pleated fabric along the length of the rope and secure each end to the rope with rubber bands, as per the standard yanagi method (see pages 94–95). Tie synthetic twine to one end of your rope and secure with a knot. Wind the twine firmly around the fabric-covered rope at random intervals. Continue down the length of the rope, tying securely at the bottom.

Place the fabric in a soaking bucket for 15 minutes. Prepare the synthetic indigo vat according to the instructions on page 18. Remove your piece from the soaking bucket and wipe off the excess water. Submerge your fabric in the dye tub for approximately 10 minutes.

Remove the fabric and allow it to oxidize for 15 minutes. Rinse the bound piece under cold water until the water runs clear, before unbinding and rinsing again.

## 3 Compressed

Through this mixture of techniques, arashi and yanagi, a new pattern is achieved with finer details and tonal variations.

Lay your fabric out flat and iron. Iron ½-inch (1-cm) knife pleats into your fabric. Wrap the pleated fabric along the length of the rope and secure each end to the rope with rubber bands, as per the standard yanagi method (see pages 94–95). Add rubber bands down the length of the rope at random intervals, compressing the fabric toward one end of the rope as you go, and securing.

Place the fabric in a soaking bucket for 15 minutes. Prepare the synthetic indigo vat according to the instructions on page 18. Remove your piece from the soaking bucket and wipe off the excess water. Submerge your fabric in the dye vat for approximately 15 minutes.

Remove the fabric and allow it to oxidize for 15 minutes. Rinse the bound piece under cold water until the water runs clear, before unbinding and rinsing again.

# Project: Yanagi apron

Decorating your old stained apron is easy, and a busy pattern like yanagi will make it an item you'll want to wear to inspire you on all your creative projects.

The traditional pattern of yanagi is delicate and fine, but by adapting the size of pleats or folds, you can modify this technique to accommodate the shape of a premade item.

**1** Lay your apron on a flat surface and iron out any creases.

**2** Iron 1-inch (2.5-cm) knife pleats into your apron.

**3** Wrap your pleated fabric along the length of the rope and secure each end to the rope with rubber bands.

**4** Tie synthetic twine to one end of the rope and secure with a knot. Wind the twine firmly around the fabric-covered rope at random intervals.

**5** Continue down the length of the rope, tying securely at the bottom.

**6** Place the apron in a soaking bucket for 30 minutes.

**7** Prepare your synthetic indigo dye vat according to the instructions on page 18.

**8** Remove your apron from the soaking bucket and wipe off the excess water with a towel. Submerge your bound apron in the dye tub for approximately 15 minutes.

**9** Remove carefully and allow to oxidize for 15 minutes.

**10** Rinse the bound piece under cold water until the water runs clear. Unbind, rinse again, and wash with dishwashing liquid.

## Traditional yanagi

In traditional Japanese yanagi, the fabric is hand gathered in tiny little pleats before being bound around the rope. It is these random hand gatherings that create the unique willow-like lines. However, in this version, an iron is used to hold the pleats in place to make the technique easier for beginners.

# Discharge bleaching

Discharge is removing color, rather than adding color. It is the reverse technique to most dyeing processes. This is exciting because you're turning shibori upside down!

A ny binding technique can be used with this process. The fabric is bound as usual, and then it is submerged in a vat of bleach rather than dye. The results will be the mirror image of what you would see if a dye vat had been used. The binding will protect the color, and the exposed fabric will be bleached.

Cellulose fiber is the most commonly used fabric for discharge bleaching, but any natural fiber that has been pre-dyed will work well. Domestic chloride bleach and commercial discharge pastes can be used. Bleach degenerates fabric, so the process must be slowed down to minimize the risk of fabric deterioration. Discharge pastes are more difficult to source and require a much more advanced process of coloring, but they are considerably more versatile because of their paste consistency and are less tough on the fabric. The concentration of bleach or discharge paste used will also influence the bleached color and consistency, as well as likely damage to the fabric.

This technique is used in fashion because of the popularity of the stressed appearance, particularly in denim jeans. Denim is an ideal material because it is a strong worker's fabric that is complemented by this technique.

Knowing discharge bleaching processes gives artists more creative power, since they are not limited to the dye colors they may have access to. A beautiful color on a fabric can be maintained and a pattern can be impressed upon it using bleach.

Due to the harsh nature of the chemicals involved in bleaching, it is advisable to undertake this process outside.

## you will need

Iron

Piece of pre-dyed natural fiber cloth (1)

Two matching resist shapes (2)

Clamps (3)

Soaking bucket

Paper mask/ respirator

Rubber gloves

Bleaching bucket

Household bleach (4)

Bleach neutralizing solution (see page 18)

**2**  **3**

# Discharging color

**1** Iron the piece of fabric, then lay it down on a hard surface.

**2** Accordion pleat the fabric horizontally into pleats of 4 inches (10 cm) by folding the fabric one way and then the other. If your aesthetic lends itself to precision, you may choose to mark out your pleat intervals with tailor's chalk.

**3** Repeat the pleat vertically to create a square shape.

**4** Place the fabric between the two matching resist shapes, lining them up perfectly on either side. Secure with clamps.

**5** Place the clamped fabric in a bucket of water to soak for 20 minutes.

**6** Fill a bucket with water and add 1 cup (250 ml) of household bleach. Submerge your presoaked piece into the bleach mix.

**7** Leave the piece to discharge for approximately 2 hours, regularly agitating until the desired tone is reached.

**8** Remove the piece from the bleach, remove the clamps, and wash thoroughly with water. Mix up your bleach neutralizing solution (1 tablespoon of sodium metabisulfite to 2½ gallons [10 L] of water). Soak your piece for 2 hours, remove, and re-rinse.

## 1 Soda ash

Soda ash, otherwise known as washing soda, is an alternative to using bleach. It is less harmful to your fabric, safer to use, and appropriate for application on hand-dyed fabrics.

Fold your pre-dyed fabric horizontally into 4-inch (10-cm) accordion pleats. Repeat the pleat vertically, making a square shape. Secure with rubber bands horizontally and vertically (this will create a cross).

Place the fabric in a soaking bucket for 20 minutes. Fill an old large cooking pot with enough water to accommodate the fabric and allow it to move freely. Set on the cooktop to boil. Add the soda ash once the water is boiling (2 tablespoons of soda ash to 2 pints [1 L] of water). Remove your fabric from the soaking bucket and submerge it into the cooktop pot. Continue boiling for approximately 1½ hours. Check the fabric regularly until the color is removed.

Once this has happened, remove the fabric with tongs, unbind, and scrub with dishwashing liquid and water (once cool enough to handle).

## 2 Boxes

This is the reverse of the boxes stitch resist method (see page 48). It is best to use a sturdy fabric such as a cotton drill, which will withstand the bleaching.

Lay your fabric out and iron. Starting from the end, fold the fabric forward 2 inches (5 cm) and then fold this forward twice more (maintaining the same width), in order to create four levels of fabric that are 2 inches (5 cm), with the excess fabric coming out of the side. Iron flat. Turn your piece to the side and accordion pleat the length of the folded fabric. Using a double-threaded needle, pass the needle through your accordion pleats to hold the gather. Knot the thread to secure.

Place the fabric in a soaking bucket for 20 minutes. Mix up your bleach solution (3½ fluid ounces [100 ml] of bleach to 1 cup [250 ml] of water). Remove the fabric from the bucket and wring out the excess water. Place it in the bucket with the bleach solution and set aside to discharge for 2 hours.

Remove the fabric with tongs, rinse thoroughly, and remove the stitches. Mix up your bleach-neutralizing solution (1 tablespoon of sodium metabisulfite to 2½ gallons [10 L] of water). Soak your piece for 2 hours, remove and rinse again.

## 3 Bleach and over-dye using Itajime triangles

This pattern acts like an echo of a former shape.

You'll need two matching flat triangle shapes for the resist. Natural-colored burlap has been used here. Fold the fabric horizontally with pleats of 4 inches (10 cm), and then fold your fabric back and forth following the line of your triangle shape.

Place your fabric between your 4-inch (10-cm) triangle resist shapes, secure with clamps, soak in warm water for 5 minutes, and then gently place in a bucket containing your bleach solution (3½ fluid ounces [100 ml] of bleach to 1 cup [250 ml] of water). Leave for 2 hours or until the color has been removed. Remove the fabric with tongs and rinse the bleach off with water. Mix up your bleach-neutralizing solution (1 tablespoon of sodium metabisulfite to 2½ gallons [10 L] of water). Undo the resists and triangle folds until the fabric is in its original pleats. Refold the triangles in a different way and place between the resists and clamps. Prepare the fiber-reactive dye by dissolving it in warm water, then add to a large dye pot filled with warm water. Add salt and soda ash. Submerge your fabric for approximately 30 minutes. Then remove, rinse under cold water, undo the clamps, and rinse again until the water runs clear.

# Project: Pink dip-bleached burlap cushion case

Mixing fabrics and textures such as burlap and playing with distressing fabric adds rustic charm.

Creating stripes with the natural color of burlap and an extra dye color can result in a versatile outdoor cushion.

1 Soak your premade burlap cushion case in a bucket of water for 30 minutes.

2 Fill a bucket with water and add 1 cup (250 ml) of household bleach. Stir thoroughly.

3 Drape two-thirds of the cushion case in the bleach solution, leaving the other end hanging over the side.

4 Leave the piece to discharge for 2 hours, agitating regularly.

5 Remove carefully from the bucket and wash thoroughly with water and dishwashing liquid, making sure no bleach is left on the burlap.

6 Prepare a tub of pink fiber-reactive dye as per the instructions on page 18. Drape the top third of your bleached section of the cushion case in the bucket. Leave for 30 minutes.

7 Remove the cushion case carefully from the bucket and rinse thoroughly with water. Mix up your bleach neutralizing solution of 1 tablespoon of sodium metabisulfite to 2½ gallons (10 L) of water and soak your bleached burlap for 2 hours. Remove from the soaking bucket and rinse again.

## Discharge tips

When using bleach to remove color, it is important to consider the fabric you are using. A strong, durable fabric like burlap or denim tolerates the bleach and gives amazing patterns and textures that are worthy of further experimentation.

If you wish to discharge a silk or more delicate cloth, consider using a discharge paste, which is a chemical activated by the use of steam. Discharge paste can be used for screen printing or fabric painting, or watered down and used with shibori to perform reverse effects on your pieces. Instead of adding color to the unbound area you are focusing on, you keep the existing fabric color and remove the surrounding color.

# Space dyeing

For many centuries, artists have spread bound cloth across a surface and poured dye concentrate onto certain areas to control the color application. Space dyeing refers to this process and is the contemporary version of this old technique that does not necessarily use bound cloth, but does use drizzling, squirting, and splashing! Fun and easy, this technique is perfect for everyone, including kids.

Space dyeing can be as simple as spreading a piece of fabric across a surface and pulling areas of it into small peaks. When the dye is poured over the fabric, the peaks will not be covered, and this creates differences in tone. This technique allows the artist to use multiple colors and plays on the integration and intermixing of these colors.

Space dyeing is like scrunch dyeing (see pages 84–89), but without the definitive lines that come from binding. The pattern is bolder and braver and makes for fantastic statement pieces. This is modern shibori at its best, informed by age-old techniques, but producing something unique, simple, and appealing in contemporary design.

This technique begins with white or lightly colored cloth, which is spread out in a shallow dye tub. Arranging damp, pre-treated fabric in raised peaks and swirls gives a ground on which the dye will be poured. Once the artist has mixed and prepared dye concentrates in the chosen color palette, it is then time to drizzle, pour, or squirt the dye in selected areas. The colors will intermingle and combine in an organic manner, and the raised peaks will remain clean or have bleeding dye tones.

Color choice is the most important design element that the artist needs to consider in space dyeing, as inappropriate color combinations can yield unwanted results. Space dyeing is the easiest of all techniques and is a great way to involve kids in the fun of tie-dye.

2

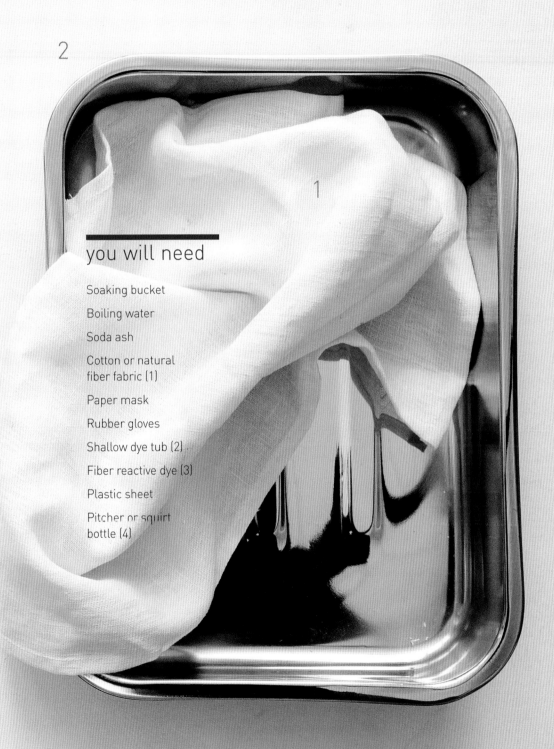

1

## you will need

Soaking bucket

Boiling water

Soda ash

Cotton or natural
fiber fabric (1)

Paper mask

Rubber gloves

Shallow dye tub (2)

Fiber reactive dye (3)

Plastic sheet

Pitcher or squirt
bottle (4)

2

4

# How to space dye your fabric

**1** Fill a bucket with boiling water and add 2 tablespoons of soda ash. Stir to dissolve.

**2** Carefully put the fabric in the bucket and leave to soak for 20 minutes, stirring occasionally.

**3** Remove the fabric from the bucket and wring out the excess water. Do not rinse.

**4** Lay the fabric in a shallow dye tub.

5

6

**5** Arrange the fabric in raised peaks and swirls, providing areas for the dye to sit.

**6** Mix up ⅔ oz (5g) of the fiber-reactive dye with ½ pint (300 ml) of warm water. Using either a squirt bottle or jug, pour the dye into the fabric folds and creases.

**7** Loosely cover with the plastic sheet and leave overnight.

**8** Remove the fabric from the dye tub and rinse under cold running water until the water runs clear.

# 1 Ice dyeing

An innovative and playful method that achieves random patterns and textures.

Freeze a number of trays of ice (enough to cover the surface area of your fabric). Dissolve 2 tablespoons of soda ash in a bucket of boiling water and soak your fabric in this for 30 minutes. Remove the fabric and wring out the excess water. Arrange the fabric with peaks and folds on an old baking rack above a shallow tray to collect the melted ice.

Take the ice cubes from the freezer and place them in the desired pattern on your fabric. Choose several complementary dye colors in powder form. Using an old spoon, sprinkle the dye powder onto the ice so that all the ice is covered. Set aside in a safe place and leave the ice to melt and the magic to happen for 24 hours.

The dye is now set, and you may rinse your fabric thoroughly in cold water until it runs clear.

# 2 Two color dyes

A super-fun process that allows for bold color statements—great for kids!

Soak your fabric in a bucket of boiling water and soda ash for 30 minutes. Remove from the soaking bucket and wring out the excess water. Lay your fabric in a shallow dye tub. Arrange the cloth in raised peaks and swirls, providing areas for the dye solutions to sit in. Mix up ⅖ oz (5g) of each of the fiber-reactive dyes with ½ pint (300 ml) of warm water and pour each color into one of the two separate squirt bottles or pitchers. Using the squirt bottles or pitchers, apply the solutions to different areas of the fabric as you desire. Cover with plastic wrap and leave overnight.

Remove and rinse under cold water until the water runs clear.

# 3 Denim

Space dyeing textures is a fun and modern way to decorate your denim with dramatic and unique results.

Lay your fabric in a shallow tub. Arrange the fabric in raised peaks and swirls, providing areas for the bleach solution to sit in. Mix up your bleach solution using 3½ fluid ounces (100 ml) of bleach to 1 cup (250 ml) of water. Using a squirt bottle or pitcher, apply the bleach solution to your fabric folds and creases. Set aside somewhere safe and leave to discharge for 2 hours. If you are not satisfied with the result after this time, mix a slightly stronger solution (e.g., 7 fluid ounces [200 ml] of bleach to 1 cup [250 ml] of water). Return the fabric to the tub until it reaches a color you are happy with.

Once complete, rinse off the bleach thoroughly. Mix up your bleach-neutralizing solution (1 tablespoon of sodium metabisulfite to 2½ gallons [10 L] of water). Soak your piece for 2 hours, remove, and rinse again.

1

2

3

# Project: Space-dyed table runner and napkins

The simple technique of space dyeing lends itself beautifully to creating a soft, watercolor-like pattern that adds a funky touch to any table setting. This project used pink, gray, and blue fiber-reactive dye.

When using multiple colors with space dyeing, it is important to choose colors that will work well when placed together.

1 Prewash your table runner and napkins before dyeing.

2 Fill a bucket with boiling water and add 2 tablespoons of soda ash. Stir to dissolve. Carefully put the runner and napkins in the bucket and leave to soak for 20 minutes, stirring occasionally.

3 Remove your items from the bucket and wring out the excess water. Do not rinse.

4 Lay your items in a shallow dye tub. Arrange the fabric in raised peaks and swirls, providing areas for the dye to sit.

5 Mix up ⅔ oz (5g) of each of the fiber-reactive dyes with ½ pint (300 ml) of warm water and pour each color into one of the four separate squirt bottles. For this design we are using four colors of fiber-reactive dye: peach pink, indigo blue, turquoise blue, and dusky gray. Using one squirt bottle at a time, pour the dye concentrate into the fabric folds and creases. Pour slowly.

6 Loosely cover with a plastic sheet and leave overnight.

7 Remove the fabric from the dye tub and rinse under cold running water until the water runs clear.

## Space-dyeing tips

Fiber-reactive dyes are the most permanent of all the dyes available. This is because of the chemical reaction that takes place when soda ash is added. This creates a chemical bond with the dye, becoming a part of the fiber molecule. Presoaking an item in soda ash before dyeing treats the fabric, creating a base for this reaction to take place.

Fiber-reactive dyes are recommended for space dyeing your table runner and napkins, as there is a huge range of vibrant colors available, and they will be sure to last a long time despite the high level of washing.

# Rust patterns

Transferring rust onto fabric to create beautiful colors and patterns is not just one of the most aesthetically pleasing techniques; it is also the most fun. Find old, rusty metals lying around in your shed and experiment!

This technique is about using rusty items as both your dye and your shape resist. There are so many different ways to use rust in dyeing. You can make clear shapes or perfect replicas on fabric that mimic the rusty item of choice, or create abstract imprints by wrapping wet fabric around items and binding in different areas. Alternative processes include submerging the bound fabric in water or resting rusty items on top of a flat, wet fabric and leaving it to dry.

This technique is less about following instructions and more about experimenting to see what you can produce. One of the most exciting things about this process is that you can make your own dye from rust. By placing old, rusty objects into water and leaving them to sit, this becomes a workable dye. Fabric can be bound using any technique in this book and then dyed with your rust concoction.

Once you are happy with the patterns on your fabric, it is important to cease the rusting process by soaking the fabric in salted water to avoid disintegration. The colors that can be achieved with rust are earthy and organic, and in tones that can rarely be replicated with synthetic dyes. This is an introduction to the world of using found objects to create your own natural dyes.

## you will need

2 pieces of white or lightly colored linen or natural fiber cloth (1)

White wine vinegar (2)

Soaking bucket

2 plastic drop cloths

Towel

Old rusted items (3)

Weights or heavy items to weigh down your items (4)

Spray bottle

Salt (5)

# How to use rust as a dye

**1** Soak the fabric in a bucket of half white wine vinegar and half water. Use enough liquid to cover the cloth fully. Leave for approximately 1 hour.

**2** Lay down one of the plastic drop cloths on a flat surface in an area that can stay undisturbed for a week. (This is the dyeing time.)

**3** Remove the fabric from the bucket, wring out, and remove the excess liquid with a towel.

**4** Place one piece of the wet fabric flat on the drop cloth. Arrange the rusted items on the fabric in an aesthetically pleasing way.

6

**5** Lay the second piece of vinegar-soaked fabric over the top of the rusted items and cover with the second plastic drop cloth.

**6** Place the weights on top of the plastic. Try to get the weight into all the crevices to achieve the best possible patterns. Leave to rest for a week.

**7** Check the piece twice a day by carefully removing the weights and lifting the plastic. Spray the fabric with vinegar if it is dry and replace the cover and weights.

**8** When you are happy with your rusted impression, remove the rusted items. Prepare a salt water solution to neutralize the rusting process by dissolving 3 tablespoons of salt per 2 pints (1 L) of water, and soak the fabric for 2 hours. Rinse under cold running water.

## 1 Wraparound rust

This technique creates an amazing abstract feature piece that texturally alludes to the shape used. Horseshoes, keys, and rusty kitchen utensils are great items to use.

Soak the fabric in a bucket containing one part white wine vinegar and one part water. Use enough liquid to cover the cloth fully. Leave for approximately 1 hour. Remove the fabric from the bucket and wring out. Wrap your fabric very tightly around your chosen rusted item and secure with rubber bands. Place on a plastic drop cloth and set aside for 24 hours if a lighter shade is desired, or 3 to 5 days for a darker shade. Spray the fabric with white wine vinegar if it dries during this time. When you are happy with your rusted shade, unwrap the fabric and remove the rusted item.

Prepare a saltwater solution to neutralize the rusting process by dissolving 3 tablespoons of salt per 2 pints (1 L) of water and soak the fabric for 2 hours. Rinse under cold running water.

## 2 Rusted stripes

You can create striped rust resists using rusted poles or metal dowels.

Soak two pieces of fabric in a bucket containing one part white wine vinegar and one part water. Use enough liquid to cover the cloth fully. Leave for about 1 hour. Lay down a plastic drop cloth on a flat surface in an area that can stay undisturbed for a week (this is the dyeing time).

Remove the fabric from the bucket and wring it out. Place one piece of the fabric flat on the plastic drop cloth. Arrange the rusted items on the fabric in your chosen design. Lay the second piece of fabric over the top of the rusted items and cover with a second plastic drop cloth. Place weights on top of the plastic.

Leave to rest for a week. Check the piece twice a day. Spray the fabric with white wine vinegar if it is dry, and replace the cover and weights. When you are happy with your rusted impression, remove the rusted items. Prepare a saltwater solution to neutralize the rusting process by dissolving 3 tablespoons of salt per 2 pints (1 L) of water and soak the fabric for 2 hours. Rinse under cold running water.

## 3 Using rust with arashi

This is a contemporary take on arashi binding.

Soak the fabric in a bucket containing one part white wine vinegar and one part water. Use enough liquid to cover the cloth fully. Leave for approximately 1 hour. Remove the fabric from the bucket and wring it out. Lay your fabric on a flat surface and place a rusted pole on one end. Roll your fabric straight around the pole and secure both ends with rubber bands. Place rubber bands down the length of the pole, compressing the fabric as you go.

Protect with plastic wrap and set aside for 24 hours if a lighter shade is desired, or 3 to 5 days for a darker shade. Spray the fabric with white wine vinegar if it dries during this time. When you are happy with your rusted shade, unwrap the fabric and remove the pole.

Prepare a saltwater solution to neutralize the rusting process by dissolving 3 tablespoons of salt per 2 pints (1 L) of water and soak the fabric for 2 hours. Rinse under cold running water.

# Project: Lucky rust horseshoe wall hanging

Rusty horseshoes make great patterns on natural linen, and experimenting with rust is a great introduction to natural dye and all its capabilities. No matter what rusted items you find around the house, it's easy to create a designer artwork that will be one of a kind and leave a lasting rusted impression.

By creating a strong geometric pattern with the rusted horseshoes you produce a stronger statement piece.

1 Soak the fabric in a bucket of half white wine vinegar and half water. Use enough liquid to cover the cloth fully. Leave for approximately 1 hour.

2 Lay a plastic drop cloth on a flat surface in an area that can stay undisturbed for a week. (This is the dyeing time.)

3 Remove the linen from the bucket, wring it out, and remove the excess liquid with a towel. Place the wet linen flat on the drop cloth.

4 Arrange the rusty horseshoes in a line on half the fabric. Fold the remaining fabric over the top of the horseshoes and cover with a second plastic drop cloth. Place weights on top of the plastic to ensure optimum rust transfer and leave to rest for a week.

5 Check your piece regularly by carefully removing weights and lifting the plastic. It could take a day or two before the rust transfers to the cloth. Spray your fabric with vinegar if it is dry, and replace the cover and weights. When you are happy with your rusted texture, move the rusted horseshoes to a new line and replace the plastic drop cloth and weights. Again, check your piece regularly and maintain the moisture. You can relay your rusty items until you feel the design is complete.

6 When you are happy with your rusty design, remove the rusted items and soak the linen in a soaking bucket filled with water and 3 tablespoons of salt. Leave for 2 hours to neutralize the rusting process, rinse with cool water, and hang out to dry.

## Rust tips

Rust is a naturally occurring phenomenon that occurs when iron reacts with oxygen, producing a beautiful burnt orange color. There are several ways to take advantage of this natural phenomenon, and rust transfer is one magical way.

It is also possible to dye over the top of the rust-dyed fabric. The natural orange color looks amazing when paired with indigo, or try over-dyeing with fiber-reactive cold-water dyes to add other complementary colors.

NOTE: Rust can weaken the fibers of your fabric, so it is recommended to use the rust-dyed cloth in projects that won't be washed often.

# Index

## Resources

**North America**
www.aljodye.com
www.dharmatrading.com
www.earthguild.com
www.gsdye.com
www.maiwa.com
www.prochemicalanddye.com

**UK**
www.thedyeshop.co.uk
www.georgeweil.com
www.kemtex.co.uk
www.omegadyes.co.uk
www.rainbowsilks.co.uk

**Australia**
www.dyeman.com
www. kraftkolour.com.au
www.shibori.com.au
www.silksational.com.au

## Credits

Quarto would like to thank Elin Noble for her
valuable editorial contribution to the book.
All step-by-step and other images are the copyright
of Quarto Publishing plc. While every effort has been
made to credit contributors, Quarto would like to
apologize should there have been any omissions
or errors—and would be pleased to make the
appropriate correction for future editions of the book.

## Authors' acknowledgments

Our thanks go out to the following people:
John Mangila, Luisa Brimble, the team at Quarto,
Leah Rauch, Lee Mathews, Sophie Trippe, the team
at Koskela, Roslyn and Jose Martin, Cameron
Haughey, Alexis Wolloff, Susan, Reuben and
Johnathan Davis, Sylvia Riley, Alena Petrikova,
and Anna Knutzelius